Little Buddha Bool

Little Buddha
Book One

Rob H. Geyer

Little Buddha Book One

Little Buddha Book One

ISBN-10: 1547273682

ISBN-13: 978-1547273683

Little Buddha Book One

Dedication

To my soul mate, the love of my life,
my wife, Maureen

and

to mother, father god
for the gift of Little Buddha

Little Buddha Book One

From the Author

I have been listening to god's voice my whole life. I've found that it comes to me in many ways, some more mysterious than others, but all of them filled with love. This book arose out of one of god's voices, which happened to be that of a small girl, Little Buddha. I feel so touched that she came to me and I hope you enjoy hearing her speak to you through the words of this book. If you'd like to contact me, my e-mail address is:

littlebuddha483@ gmail.com.

Blessings to you,
Rob

Little Buddha Book One

Table of Contents

Little Buddha Book One

Table of Contents Exercises

Little Buddha Book One

forgiveness

Little Buddha Book One

forgiveness

A small girl was standing at the water's edge. She had a little green plastic shovel and a little green plastic bucket. When a wave came toward her, she would bend down and scoop up as much water as the shovel would hold. As the waves rushed back out to the sea, she'd pour the shovel full into her bucket. It didn't matter whether the bucket was already full or not, so sometimes the water just splashed onto the sand. It was a curious enough thing that I had to ask her about it. I moved closer to her and called over, "Why are you pouring water into the bucket when it is already full?" She called back, "Why do anything?" I admit that I stared at her and couldn't think of a thing to say. Some six-year-old had just shut me up with three words.

The next morning, she was there again, but standing a few feet out into the water. Same green shovel, same green bucket. This time the bucket was submerged and of course full of water. I watched as she tried to scoop water out of the bucket in a useless attempt to empty it. I couldn't control myself, so again I called over to her, "Why are you trying to empty the bucket while it's under water?" She smiled at me with bright eyes. She was mesmerizing.

2

Little Buddha Book One

"Why not?", was the Little Buddha's reply. Again, I could think of nothing to say.

I walked back to my towel on the beach and thought about these two "conversations". Weren't the two answers opposite? Two different days, two different ideas? Indeed, why do anything and why not do anything? I wondered if really, they were the same thing, just located on a different spot on the great continuum of ideas. She seemed so wise, despite her age. I thought, maybe she doesn't know what she's talking about. Maybe she just gave me some six-year-old wise-guy response. It occurred to me to ask her a troublesome question from my life, if I ever saw her again.

Day three and there she was sitting on the beach. Her green bucket was tucked between her knees and was resting flat against the sand. Her green shovel sat behind her. The pail was completely empty and she was peering inside. I came over to stand next to her. "Why are you looking into your empty bucket?", I asked. She looked up at me quizzically and responded, "Why do you say it's empty?" I immediately wondered, what's going to be next with this child? I could see quite clearly, there wasn't anything in the little bucket. "Because it IS empty", I finally said. She laughed a beautiful warm knowing laugh and said to me, "You just need to look more closely and then you'll see. Maybe you're just out of practice. Lean down so you can see better. See the sunshine going all the way to the bottom?" She held it up for me to see. "Put your hand in here and move it all around. Do you feel all the air that moves? Put it up to your ear and listen to all the sounds you can hear". Of course, she was right, and I was wrong. Again.

"Do you think you could answer a question for me," I asked a little timidly? "Perhaps," she said. "Well, I was wondering if you could tell me about forgiveness. Do you know anything about that, even though you're so young?" I admit, I thought I was being foolish asking, but in light of her wisdom and my lack of it, I didn't see how I had anything to lose. She sat for a minute or so filling the bucket to the top with dry white sand.

"Can you imagine something," she asked? "Sometimes I have a hard time with that but I'll try hard", I responded. "OK", she said, "Imagine that my bucket is you. It's everything you think and feel and experience during your life. Imagine that everything that is within you-

4

YOU chose to put there. Nothing got in without your choosing. Nothing. Whether conscious or not, every thought, feeling, idea, reaction and prejudice. Every cruel word, every kind gesture, every act of faith, every indifference, everything. Imagine that each of these things takes up space, just like the grains of sand in my bucket. Once it's full it's very hard to find more space for anything, no matter how valuable or important. There are ways you can empty part of your bucket if you choose. One way is forgiveness. But first you have to imagine one more thing. Can you imagine that everyone else here is just like you? They've lived their lives filling their buckets and sometimes they don't have any space left either. They're doing the best they can with what weighs them down. In their hearts, they too wish to be free and to have open space to experience more of the beautiful things in life. But they too don't know how.

They probably sense it, dream about it and desperately want it just like you do. This is very important to know. To forgive anyone anything, requires YOU make a conscious choice. No one else can do it for you." She eyed me carefully saying, "Now bring to mind something which begs forgiveness. Feel the space it holds within you. The weight of it, the size, color and dimension. Imagine knowing it needn't exist and that you can fill its space with something beautiful. Now, close your eyes. Welcome it in. Let it rest in front of you. Believe that it has served its full purpose for you, but does so no longer. Look inside your heart and allow love and compassion to open within. Breathe easily. Smile for a moment. Know that no matter what, this decision is up to you and no one else. Picture your love and compassion surrounding you and the focus of your forgiveness. Now, allow it to fade and fade and fade until it disappears. Breathe and feel the space inside you open. Feel the sunshine enter you and the air move around you. Listen for the sound of your own being. Sense the room created inside of you, now open for that which does serve you. For beauty. For wholeness."

I was stunned. I wondered about her words. I wondered too where they had come from. How could a six-year-old know all of this? I considered asking, but she must have anticipated my question. She put her little hand on my arm and I could feel the warmth of her touch. It felt almost electric. "I know what your question is", she said. "It's the same one everyone asks me. It all has to do with my mother. Since I was a baby, she's taught me about the value of space. The space within each of us and the space outside of each of us. She taught me how to choose what to allow in and how to release what no longer serves me. When you have that kind of freedom, there is room for wisdom, even if you're only six." Of course, I just stood there. My first reaction was to doubt this explanation. It didn't fit with anything I'd ever experienced. Every six-year-old I'd ever known was only interested in playing, eating and sleeping. Was it time for me to break this mold? Was it time for me to learn whenever I found a teacher, no matter what their age? I looked at her. What a beautiful child, what a wise spirit. "I am so thankful to you. Is there anything I can do for you?"

She simply smiled and said, "Save me some space" and ran off with her little green shovel and little green bucket.

Little Buddha Book One

connecting the dots

Little Buddha Book One

connecting the dots

It's summer again and here I am at the beach. I've looked all over for her. I've come at different times, but I haven't seen her yet. I have so many questions for her. Finally, I've decided to change my route to the beach. There are so many narrow sandy alleyways to choose from. I guess I'll try a new one each day- the good old "trial and error" method. Who knows, maybe it will work.

I wonder if I'll even recognize her. Maybe she's changed a lot. Maybe I have too. Today I'm trying a new alleyway. The cottages that border this path are rambling houses with big green yards.

Wait, I think I see someone who could be her. My heart starts to pound and my breath is suddenly shallow. A girl, who could be eight is lying under a large colorful beach umbrella. She's mostly covered in a towel. From the little I can see of her, she seems very white, not tanned like the last time I saw her. I feel strongly drawn toward her. She's been sort of facing away from me, but has rolled over and is staring at me now. All doubt has been erased. It's her. But she doesn't look well. It's something in her eyes and her faded smile.

Little Buddha Book One

"Please don't," she says softly.

"Don't what?", I ask, wondering already what she sees inside of me.

"Don't be sad or angry or worried."

I confess I was instantly all these things. Who isn't in the presence of what appears to be some kind of serious illness. I could see the signs. Ones I knew all too well.

"Please just come in and sit with me."

So, I opened the gate, walked across the yard and stood near her. There was a noise from inside the house and a voice, "Honey, who is that?"

Little Buddha answered, "Remember the man I told you about from the beach, he's here for a visit." And from the distance, a response, "Okay honey, let me know if you need anything."

"Thanks Mom," she said.

Little Buddha looked up at me with those still beautiful eyes. She asked me to sit in the chair opposite her. "I told my Mom you'd be stopping by today, so she was kind of expecting you. Can you stay for a while?"

I assured her I could. I told her I'd been searching for her and that I wanted to talk with her and see how she was doing. It took a moment for it to dawn on me. "What do you mean you told your Mom I'd be stopping by? How did you know that?"

"You are not the only one who knows things", she said. What did that mean? I was about to ask when she said, "How did you find me?" I answered, "I just kept looking, you know, trial and error." She looked at me, "Is that what you really think?"

It seemed that every conversation with her was like this. I would start somewhere, only to have her guide me somewhere else. I figured I'd better ask my biggest question before things got totally out of hand. "Is there a plan here?", I blurted out. "You know, something that someone set up for each of us?" Before she could respond, I added, by way of apology, "I don't know where my manners are. How are you feeling? Is there anything I can do for you?"

Little Buddha Book One

She gazed at me. I've never felt so loved. What a divine face.

She startled me by speaking, "That's better...you're more relaxed now. You do not have to worry about me. My spirit soars, just like those kites out there. Yes, my body appears to have lost its harmony, but Michael is helping me."

I wondered who Michael was; her father, her brother, perhaps her doctor. She stopped my mind from wandering. "No," she said, "he's none of these. He's a friend. He's twelve and he's a 'lightgiver'."

Okay now I'm really confused. First, can she read my mind? How did she know I was thinking about who Michael was? And second, what is a 'lightgiver' anyway? And come to think of it, shouldn't I know this little girl's name by now? My face must have given all of this away because she watched me and waited patiently for me to focus on her again.

"Michael is my friend. He knows a lot about the light, what you would call 'life'. He came to show me another way to understand wellness, a better way. He is also my cousin."

Little Buddha Book One

"What do you mean, 'a better way'?"

"Well, my doctor says that I must fight and never give up and never give in. But Michael says there is another way. He says that everything we think, feel and say is either from love or from fear. He says that fear is not REAL. It is there for us to push against and to point the way toward love. It is our choice. So, if we choose to fight our condition, like my sickness, we are feeding it fear and this always creates conflict. And when your energy is already low, any kind of fighting works against you. Michael says that when you are sick and you are forced to slow down, if you look, you can see things as they are. This can be an enormous gift, because when you look closely at things it can change your perspective and allow you to see the 'DOTS' so they become meaningful to you. Michael says that love is the key. Not always easy, but always right. Love creates harmony in the body and in life. He says, 'the light' is filled with love. He works with me so that, I see how my life is about 'connecting the dots' with love."

"I'm sorry," I said, "I don't even begin to understand what you're talking about. What 'DOTS'?"

13

"It's like this," she responded. "Imagine your life is a series of pictures. Each moment is captured on a page of its own and when you put them all together they form a whole picture. Think of each of the pictures as DOTS."

I looked at her still not understanding. When I glanced over at her, she seemed to be falling asleep.

"I'm really tired right now. Can you come back tomorrow for another visit?"

"Yes, of course. I'm sorry to have tired you out. Would the morning be best?"

"Yes, that would be good", and then she added, "there's something I'd like you to do for me."

"Sure," I responded.

"You see that book on the table over there?" I reached over and picked it up. It was one of those children's activity books where there are a bunch of numbered dots on the page and after you connect them, they form a picture. She said, "Pick any page you like and follow the dots to make a picture, then bring it back

14

with you tomorrow." It seemed kind of an odd request, but I would do anything for her, so I assured her I would.

As her eyes were about to close I reached over and lightly touched her head. "See you tomorrow."

Her voice was soft in response, "Claire. My name is Claire." Somehow that seemed so right to me. "Goodbye for now Claire, sleep well."

Once I was back at my cottage I leafed through the book trying to pick a picture that appealed to me. Finally, I settled on one and took a pencil and followed the numbers in order and violá: a horse appeared on the page. That was easy, I thought.

It's the next day now and I'm excited to see her again. I hope she's feeling better today. I thought about her a lot last night and considered all the things she told me. About love and fear. No one had ever explained it that way to me before.

I'm turning down her path and am standing in front of her gate. I look over the top but can't see her. From inside the house I hear her voice. "Come in Sam." How did she know my name I wondered? Maybe I'll ask her later.

"Hi Claire. How are you today?", I call out as I come through the gate. "Heavenly," she says as she skips into the yard to greet me. "Did you do your picture?", she asks eagerly. "Yes, here it is. What do you think?"

"Very nice," she says as she lays it on the table. She picks up a book and hands it to me. "I have another one for you to do."

I open the book and look at the first page. There are dots scattered all over the page but no numbers. Same thing on the next page and the next. In fact, all of the pages in the book are the same. I don't get it. I look at her. She's smiling at me. She's on the edge of laughter and her eyes are dancing.

"How am I supposed to make a picture out of any of these? There aren't any numbers to follow."

"Ahhhh," she says, "that's a very good question."

"Thank you, so what's the answer?"

Little Buddha Book One

"Well, it's different for each person. You see, your 'horse' picture is going to look pretty much exactly like everyone else's horse picture. But the way you connect the unnumbered dots will look different from everybody else's. There is no set pattern, so every choice, every connection you make, alters the picture. Without numbers to follow it can seem meaningless. No matter the number of dots you connect, it doesn't reveal a picture to you, so, you don't see that EVERYTHING in your life is connected."

I look blankly at her. "I'm lost," I say. "Maybe if you gave me an example I might get it."

She gazes sympathetically at me. "Can you think of a significant event in your life and bring it to mind?"

I think for a moment. What do I consider "significant?" The first event that comes to me was when I lost my job. That was certainly pretty traumatic. So, I tell her about it.

"Great example," she says, "so full of promise. Okay, so now close your eyes and breathe easily…softly. Good. Now gently allow your mind to see your life just before you lost your job. Let your heart help you recall by 'feeling'

17

what was happening. Stay right here till something comes to you."

I feel very relaxed. I can see things that happened before I was told about my job loss, but without the stress I felt at the time. It is like I am hovering above it all. I can see how my stress was affecting my family and how it was making me sick. I can feel the FEAR taking over my whole body, my whole life.

Somehow, I hear her soothing voice saying, "I sense that you are experiencing many thoughts and feelings. Can you see any actual events?"

"Yes," I respond, "I can see there were lots of arguments with my family and friends."

"And what did you feel?"

"FEAR. I felt really afraid because my job was not going well and I was afraid about how I would provide for my family if I lost it. I also got sick a lot, which wasn't like me."

"Okay, so now you see the BEFORE…let's move to AFTER you lost your job. Remember to keep breathing gently and softly. Relax your mind and see what comes to you now."

Little Buddha Book One

I move forward in time. What had happened? I can see it now, once I look beyond the initial shock. There it was, a huge sense of relief, to be free from the job stress…but of course there was a new stress. Now I had to find another job. How was I going to do that? In that moment, I began to realize what Little Buddha was talking about. The way I got my next job was because a friend of mine told me about a position that had just opened up. I see what she's talking about. HE was a DOT. A connecting link in my life. I'd never thought about this before, but it was true. What other DOTS were there? What about the fear I'd had about the job I lost, was there a DOT there? I remembered what Little Buddha told me that Michael said. The purpose of fear is to give us something to push against and to point the way toward love. And that it is my choice. So maybe the DOT was that my fear created an opening for me, even though I didn't recognize it at the time. WOW! This feels really important to me.

Somewhere far outside of me I hear her voice. "Sam. Sam. Come back and gently open your eyes."

It takes me a minute, but I open my eyes, and stare at her. "Wow," I say. "Is everything in my whole life connected like this?"

"Yes," she responds. "Everything."

"But why haven't I ever noticed this before? It could make so much difference to me, to how I see life, to how I live my life."

"All things happen when you are ready and not before." And she continues, "You can see that there are DOTS now and know that each one is connected. It's actually even more amazing than this because your DOTS are connected to everyone else's DOTS."

"What?" I say in total surprise. "Are you really saying that my DOTS are connected to EVERYONE else's on earth?"

"Yes, is that hard for you to accept? Do you not see that you and I are connected? Do you think it was just a random event between us at the beach and now here at this cottage?"

My mind is reeling. I know she is right, but it is just so much to take in. Yes...I can see that she and I are connected. I can see now how events in my life are connected and that meaning comes out of every one of them, despite whether I labeled them "good" or "bad". I can see how each of them could lead me forward. What would it be like if I understood them AS they happened instead of well after the fact? 'Incredible,' that's how it would feel. And what would it be like if I understood that FEAR is actually a beautiful messenger, meant to lead me toward the light? This could change everything for me.

I love this little girl so much for connecting me with her wisdom. "Thank you so much," I say.

"You are most welcome." she responds. "Now I have a question for you."

"Oh boy." I wonder what she could possibly expect me to answer for HER.

She looks straight at me. "So, what do you think is the answer to the first question you asked me?"

At this point I can't even remember my "first" question. Oh yes, it was whether there was a plan here on earth. All I can think about was the page of scattered unnumbered dots. She said everyone connects their dots in their own way BUT that everyone's dots are connected to each other. How can that be true?

"I truly don't know the answer," I say.

"Hmmm," she says. "Do you need to know?"

I take a big breath in and respond, "No, I don't any more. It's really enough for me to know that LOVE is the answer. Not always easy, but always right."

A smile creases her face, "How divine," she says.

heaven on earth

Little Buddha Book One

heaven on earth

It's a month later and Little Buddha is much stronger. The color in her face has turned from white to pink, with a little bit of tan on her cheeks. She's as bright and happy as ever. What a marvelous light she is to me and to the world.

We've been talking a lot and she's been giving me a ton of assignments. Some seemed easy at first, but I should have known better. I would ask her questions, and she would always make me answer them first before she would tell me what she thought. I was getting used to this until one day something changed.

She told me she wanted to know what I wanted most from my life. I don't think I'd ever really thought about this. Of course, there were lots of things I wanted; food, a nice house, clothes that felt good, lots of money so I could do fun things, family who loved me. Why did I put family at the end of the list? Family was very important to me. It should have been first. I'd said this out loud to her and she frowned at me.

"What?" I said.

"You know what," she responded. "You used

that word again. Haven't we been talking about that a lot?"

I looked down and away from her. "Yes," I admitted, "you're right. I keep forgetting".

She looked at me and smiled. "Sam, words matter. The ones you say and the ones you think. When you say 'should' you are judging yourself and sometimes others too. And before you said it, you thought it. That means it's deep inside of you where it will hurt the most."

"I know," I said.

Little Buddha was still smiling. "This is for your own good you know".

Ohhh, I hated that saying, but somehow, I think she knew that. I'm sure she could tell by the look on my face. When I was a kid people used to say that to me all the time and it always made me angry.

"Have you carried that long enough?"

"What?", I said, taken aback by her question. "Carried what long enough?"

"Those feelings, the ones you just felt again."

She was always doing this to me, knowing

what was going on inside me and bringing it out in the open. It was sort of annoying.

Claire looked at me. "Oh, and now you're annoyed on top of all of your other feelings. You don't seem to want to give yourself a break."

I stayed quiet a moment. She was right, as usual. It wasn't that she was doing anything to me, except maybe telling me the truth. She'd seen that I was reacting in my normal patterns. Whenever I was questioned I went into 'protection mode'. I couldn't be 'wrong' after all. Wasn't I entitled to my emotions? If I wanted to feel hurt and be stubborn wasn't that my choice? I paused. Here I was again, in this cycle of moving from one negative, hurtful thought to the next. We'd talked about this situation a hundred times I think. Maybe more. And I still didn't get it. I just kept repeating the same behavior.

"Calm," she said. "Please take a breath and slow down. It's okay. It took you a very long time to create this cycle, and it may take you awhile to change it. Be nice to yourself. Remember how important it is for you to feed yourself love. Remember too that anything you made can be remade. Whenever you start to feel the feelings you have right now, ask yourself, 'what would benefit me?' That's the key."

"You make it sound easier than it is", I stated, somewhat defensively.

"Everything is easy by its nature. We're the ones who make it hard. But we don't have to. We can choose a different way."

"Okay," I said, "so how do you do that? I mean, you seem so at peace with the world. What's your secret?"

"There is no real secret," she said. "It's simple. I start each day when I wake up by reminding myself who I am. I am a part of god. A divine spirit, complete and whole. I am not missing anything. My reality is that I am made of love. I remind myself that everything around me is also made of love and that the only difference between me and all that surrounds me is my perception or the way I choose to see the world. If I think or act or say something that is not from love - my perception will be that I am separate from the world. And then I will label things. They can become "bad" things or "wrong" things. But if I remember that everything is a part of the one- then I can look at everything through the eyes of love. You see, the idea is simple. It is the true perceiving that is difficult."

"That sounds great, but I can't do that. I've tried, but I can't pull it off. Knowing this is the truth, but not being able to look at things the way you do is frustrating to me."

"I know," she sympathized. "It takes a lot of practice. I have a thought about what might help."

"Really," I said, "I'd love to hear it."

I could tell this wasn't going to be as easy as I'd like. Hmmm, I guess I had to admit, at least to myself, I was always looking for the easy way. I wondered why that was. I started to think about that when I felt a tap on my forehead. "What?", I said.

"You were drifting again, so I thought I'd bring you back." She had a wicked grin on her face.

"You enjoyed that, didn't you?"

She gazed at me, and I felt something beyond any love I'd ever felt. "What I enjoy is YOU," she said softly. This must be what it feels like to be a part of god - like she was telling me a couple minutes ago. No wonder she saw things beyond what I did.

"Okay," she said, "so here's a question for you. Have you ever thought about how you would like things to be?"

"Sure, all the time," I answered, somehow knowing this wasn't an answer she would accept.

"I didn't mean how you'd like them to be just for you. I mean how you'd like them to be in the world."

Now that, I had never done and she could sense it by my silence. What did it matter really? I had a hard-enough time coming up with what I wanted for myself, how was I ever going to decide what I wanted for the world?

"If you don't know what you desire, how do you think it will ever happen?", she asked.

"Wait a minute," I said. "Are you saying I can have whatever I desire? How can that ever happen? I mean really, if I want something, that means someone else can't have it too." A lot more questions were coming up in my mind. I didn't see how she was going to be able to answer them all.

She looked at me. "Take a breath," she said. So, I did. She kept looking directly at me. "Did the breath you just took mean I couldn't take a breath?"

What a ridiculous question I thought. "No, of course not, why do you ask?"

"Well," she said, "because, you said that if you wanted something, that meant someone else couldn't have it too."

"I wasn't talking about breathing."

Her eyes crinkled when she spoke next, "What about forgiveness? Or, what about love? If you want these or give these, does it limit anyone else from forgiving or loving?"

"No," I said, "but those are intangible things. I was talking about 'stuff', you know, like houses, cars and money."

"I see," she responded. "So, are those the things you most want for you and for the world?"

I had to think about that. I could hear some inner voice saying 'no' because they don't really create happiness, which is really what I want. I thought a bit more. Maybe the difference was between what my head wanted and what my heart wanted. It occurred to me that all of the things my head wanted ultimately didn't make me happy, sort of like a week-old

Little Buddha Book One

Christmas toy, but that the things my heart wanted actually did make me happy- when my head stayed out of it.

I realized she was watching me again.

"I wonder if you'd be willing to take some time and write down what you really and truly most want. Let's call it your 'heaven on earth' assignment."

I was quiet and sat slowing my breath for a minute. I sensed how important this assignment could be for me. "How long do I have to complete this?", I asked.

"As long as you need. Life isn't a race, it's a journey toward bliss."

I hugged her goodbye for the day and told her I'd be back once I was done.

It's a week later now. I was surprised how fast some parts of it came to me and how hard other parts were to open to. When I was finally done, I was really happy with it. I walked to Claire's cottage at the beach and found her sitting in the sun. She looked up when she heard me open the gate. She had the most beautiful smile aimed in my direction. "It's so nice to see you Sam. I can't wait to hear your story." She beckoned me to sit by her. "So," she said looking expectantly at me.

"Okay," I said, "here it is, my essay on life, called - Heaven on Earth."

Heaven on Earth assignment:

My first thought/feeling is that you would be able to hug another person for as long as it took to feel balanced- that you could send love outward to them and receive love in from them- and all of this would be considered normal- that it would be so filling, rewarding, enlivening that everyone would want to do it- that it would not get confusing for anyone.

And

We could all say to each other, "I love you" and it would feel "right"- there wouldn't be awkwardness or uncomfortable expectations attached- that saying it would be an extension of our hearts recognizing, appreciating and connecting with each other.

And

We would feel free to give each other gifts- both large and small and it would happen spontaneously, from a center of love, not based only on acceptable events, but anytime- the gifts would not have to be equaled or paid back, they would feel good to receive and perhaps we could gain a sense of comfort with the concept that there will always be enough for everyone if we share from the heart.

And

We could touch each other because we care and want to support and enrich each other's lives, because we realize that it is just as important and necessary as when we were first born to be held and caressed and know we mean something to someone- that we would realize that touch fills our life with love, creates connection, expands our hearts, increases our immunity, focuses us outward, gives life and creates life.

And

We would know the beauty of giving from a calm, generous, loving heart- which raises up the giver as it supports the receiver, we'd know it is beautiful to be both giver and receiver, that it balances us, connects us- that we could give without thought of need of receiving, but just for the pure joy giving contains within itself- that we would grow in opening our hearts till it became our nature, our first action, our expanding from love.

Little Buddha Book One

And

We would see how forgiveness sets us free and invites others to do the same- we would open to know that everyone hurts, everyone lacks, everyone needs, everyone is in pain and that their unkind actions come from these lacks- from the lack of love, such that only love can fill their empty space- and forgiveness is born from love, the kind of love that recognizes the choice of sacrificing our own sense of pain to fill another with love- and surprisingly, in the process we are also healed.

And

We would find that "community" happens naturally when we touch, hug, care, love and forgive each other- and that once we build community there will always be support for all of us- no one would ever have to feel alone or separate, that there would always be someone to help, to comfort, to teach, to encourage our dream, to reward our contribution, to love us.

And

There would be abundant and gentle humor, not filled with anger, envy or harm- a kind of humor that includes, rather than excludes- a kind of humor that joins us in laughter and connection- a kind of humor that increases joy.

And

There would be creativity of all kinds; art, music, writing, building- and everyone would be encouraged to participate, no matter what their skill level was because creativity is individual and it would grow in a loving environment- where imagination would be given life and seen as an extension of heaven to be appreciated- a place where you could lose yourself in abandon.

And

It would be a place of "potential peace", sometimes utterly peaceful where everything is at joyful rest; balanced, centered, open, deliriously right and when the world turns to chaos, fear, anger, worry and hurt, there would exist an awareness that peace is still possible, and people would see those in pain and come to their aid, to listen, to hold them, to help them release their fears, to touch their spirit and show their love and in this act, provide balance for both giver and receiver- a kind of sacred harmony.

And

There would be a feeling of freedom within

each of us, a certain knowing that we are loved, wholly and completely by the divine- so that there would always be a center of hope within us, a light that cannot be extinguished, a flame that kindles our own love and that connects us to everyone else, our sacred family- so that joy is always present.

I looked over at her. She was crying, tears streamed down her face. "That was beautiful. Thank you so much. I feel so blessed to know you and hear you." She came over to me and hugged me. I felt so at home.

Little Buddha Book One

the inner path-beginning

Little Buddha Book One

the inner path-beginning

It's almost the end of summer now. I've had such inspiring talks with her and learned so much. I wonder sometimes what she sees in me to spend so much time with me. She's sitting opposite me at the moment. Beautiful as ever.

I've finished all of my "assignments" and am beginning to believe in my own wisdom and that I might have something worth sharing with others. I must have said this out loud because I hear her voice.

"Of course, you know it all", she says.

I can't help asking, "Now that's going a bit too far isn't it?"

"After this whole summer, you still want to put limits on yourself?", she responds.

I look at her. "I can't help it. I feel like there is still so much for me to learn."

She shrugs, "We all feel that way."

"But you always seem to know everything," I say.

"That's because I ask and then follow the path inside of me."

I have to pursue this. "What path? Can you show me the way?"

She smiles at me. Even after all of this time, it melts me. She seems to be considering something before she answers. Finally, she says, "I can point you toward the way, but I can't show you the way. You have to do that yourself."

Clearly there is some deep meaning to her answer. She could "point" the way but not "show" me the way. I wonder what the difference is. I also wonder if there will ever come a time when I understand her without some further explanation. After a minute, I ask, "What do you mean you can point the way but not show me the way?"

"Each of knows the way. We've always known the way, but we chose to forget, so that everything here can be experienced. I can point the way by suggesting some things that will help you see for yourself, but you have to show yourself the truth."

Little Buddha Book One

As usual, I don't have a clue what she really means and I tell her so.

"Okay Sam, imagine we're in a very dark cave. We're standing next to each other and you ask me how we're going to find our way out. Because I've been in the cave before I tell you that you go straight then take a left and a right and you will find the cave opening. Would you go?"

"I don't think so," I say, "because I'd probably bang into the cave walls and hurt myself."

"Okay, so suppose I handed you a flashlight, then would you go?"

"Sure, because now you've told me the directions and I can see where I'm going."

"Well, my directions are 'pointing the way' and you holding the flashlight is you 'showing yourself the way'."

I guess that makes sense, but I still want the flashlight. That's the trouble with some of her answers, they make sense but I need more. I know that she thought I could always work it out, but just once I'd have loved a straight answer. Why did this have to be so hard?

"Ow," I say. She'd tapped me on the forehead again. I've lost track of the number of times she'd done that. I must have drifted off again.

"Sam, you're trying too hard. This is easy stuff."

"Maybe for you it is."

She gazes at me. "Do me a favor", she says, "without 'thinking' about this first, tell me what you 'feel' we're talking about."

"We're talking about how I can find my inner path, like you've found yours. I get that our paths are probably different and that you can only help me, not do it for me." I pause considering what to add. I'm wondering, why an 'inner path'? Can't I get to where I want to go by learning things that are outside of me? Doesn't the world have enough wisdom to teach me? Probably a lot more than could possibly be 'inside' of me. I look at her. She is smiling at me again. "What?" I say.

"Why do you trust the wisdom outside of you and not the wisdom inside of you?", she asks.

"Because that's what I've been taught my whole life," I respond, thinking to myself, isn't that the way it is for everyone?

"But Sam," she says, "haven't we been talking all summer about how we all limit ourselves? And isn't this just another of those limits? When you assume that all wisdom is on the outside, you can't see the value of all that is on the inside."

I think I get her point, but I guess I don't really trust that I have anything inside me, except what I've learned from others. Maybe I need another example.

"Can you tell me a story about what you mean?"

"Sure," she says. "Once there was a farmer who lived in a very dry climate. He desperately needed water for his crops because selling them supported his life and that of his family. He'd tried every method he could think of; diverting a nearby creek, catching the little rainwater that fell, even paying for cloud seeding to make it rain. Nothing worked. Finally, he decided to try something a friend told him about. So, he hired a 'diviner', someone who supposedly could hold a special stick and walk his property and tell him exactly the location of water underground. Once the farmer knew the location of the water, he could dig a well and irrigate his crops. He wasn't sure it would work, but felt he had to try. So, he hired the diviner, who came and walked the property and at one particular location suddenly stopped. His stick was bobbing up and down and finally came to rest pointing at the ground. The diviner looked at the farmer and told him this was the spot. Although doubtful, the farmer thanked and paid the diviner. The next day the farmer and his two sons dug and dug. Nothing. No water. The farmer threw down his shovel in disgust and stomped off toward his house. His sons decided they would dig a bit further. It was hard work and the hole was getting so deep they needed a ladder to get in and out. At one point, one of the sons jumped off the ladder before reaching the bottom rung and felt the earth give way a bit. He looked down and saw water pooling around his boots. He yelled up to his brother, 'Water!'. They both shouted with joy."

Well, this wasn't the example I was thinking of. In fact, I was having a hard time making any sense of it. "What does this have to do with my question?", I ask.

"Sam, you told me that you felt you could only trust wisdom on the outside of you. That you didn't believe you had any inner wisdom. Right?"

"Yes," I respond.

"Well, you're like the farmer, who although he was desperately seeking an answer to his dilemma, like your quest for wisdom, he doubted anything but that which was on the outside. He distrusted the inner wisdom that guided the diviner. And not only that, he gave up easily and if it were not for his two sons, would never have found water."

"Are you saying the farmer lacked faith in the process and that was the problem?"

"No, although that is true, the really important part of the story is the faith of the diviner. He believed, he knew that something inside of him would connect with something inside of the earth, telling him exactly where the presence of water was. You see, he was following his inner path, his divine connection."

"So, what are you saying? I know you are always telling me about the power of 'choosing' and how that affects my whole life.

Are you saying that to find my own inner path is just another choice?" I am really feeling fuzzy and unsure. Frankly, I need some reassurance that I will ever get this straight.

She takes my hands in hers and asks me to close my eyes and breathe, slowly, in and out. To picture the blue of the ocean and feel the cool breeze and smell the salty scent in the air. And when she can tell I am calm and centered, she speaks these words, "You've spent your entire life focused outward, believing everything could be revealed to you through the words and observations of others. You've been told that wisdom is obtained through school and books and jobs and from smarter people than you. You've been conditioned to learn facts and build on them in the hope that one day you would become wise and know what path to travel. But the truth, as I know it, is that everything of importance is within you already. The divine creation exists inside of every person. It has always been there. I feel certain that at times you've experienced this, like a bubbling up around your feet, like the water in the farmer's well. And you just know the answer to questions. You sense the breakthroughs you need and the direction you would be wise to take. I know that you've been told that wisdom is a process of acquisition, but I'm telling you, it is the opposite. My inner path has become a beautiful process of releasing all my assumptions about everything. As I let go, what I realize is that there is a divine wisdom at my very core. As I release what I 'think' I know, I can 'feel' the truth. Sometimes my inner path is quiet, a serene oasis far beyond the noise of this world. But it is also true, that even during the stress filled storms within my life, I experience an awareness of my truth, beyond any earthly wisdom."

I look at her. She is radiant and there is a glow around her that seems to shimmer. I don't feel that I completely understand all of what she is telling me, but I know it is important for me to stay with it. "I'm still a little confused. What I hear you telling me is that there is an innate inner wisdom everyone possesses and that if you can connect with this, there is clarity and wisdom that can guide your life."

"Yes, that's what I've come to realize", she answers.

What I wanted to know now was 'how'. How could I get in touch with my own inner wisdom, with the divine inside of me, so I ask, "Claire, I know this works for you, but how can this work for me?"

She stares at me for a moment before answering. It feels like she was considering what to tell me. "Do you remember my telling you that we knew everything but we chose to forget, so that we could fully experience this world? Well, this may not sound important, but it is. It's the key to everything. Hidden inside of you is every answer you could ever want or need. To move from the outside to the inside releases every limit and opens the whole world to you. Choosing to remember is like turning on the flashlight when you are in the cave of darkness."

I am trying hard to see what she is saying but I need a little more help. "Are you saying that everyone of us has the ability to know everything, to 'remember' it, rather than having to 'learn' it?"

"Yes. Imagine you're sitting comfortably in a chair looking out at the ocean. You see the surf rolling toward and landing on the beach and feel the warmth of the sun. You see the gulls soaring and spinning through the air and hear their piercing cries. You're totally absorbed in this scene unaware that there is a

47

Little Buddha Book One

thin veil between all that you see and another truth that exists. A truth, that beyond your earth perceptions there is a divine space, a place you know even better than this world. A place you first called home, a space called 'heaven'. Allow yourself the freedom to feel this place and rest here for a minute. Allow yourself to remember. Feel your heart open and fill with joy. Stay right here and feel refreshed and renewed."

I am blissfully lost within this world she has guided me toward. I used her words to light the way. It is true, I did see beyond everything I thought was the only truth and the only thing I had ever known. Fantastic! Pure delight and wonder, beyond my ability to even describe.

I have no idea how long we sat together, entranced in this new world. Somehow, I do remember opening my eyes. It took a while for things to come back into focus. "Wow", I say, "that was awesome. I am so thankful, so utterly amazed and thankful. Is that what you've been talking about all this time?"

"Yes. You can now see that there is more than you've ever been taught. That any sort of limits, are only your perceptions- choices you've accepted. You can sense that there is a truth which is undeniable, one that is filled with bliss."

She smiles and gazes into my eyes. And I can see in them the same truth I have just seen inside of me. I didn't understand how this was possible, but still I saw it. She and I are from the same place. I wonder, is it this way with everyone. I wonder too if I can find my way back.

She is smiling even brighter than before, and says, "Sam, you know the truth now and you can always find your way back by remembering what this felt like. Release your doubts and let them fall away and disappear. Embrace your new truth. Take it fully into your heart, your whole body. Know that you can, that you do, live connected to the source of all love. Spend time inside this connection. This is what lies within your inner path. It is always present, always divine, always available. And always remember, if you need help, ask and you will be answered."

the bug box

Little Buddha Book One

the bug box

It's been a whole year since I've seen her. We've communicated through letters, actual paper folded neatly into an envelope. She prefers letters. She says they are 'old school' and they carry the vibration of the writer. She says it helps to feel what the author feels, to see their words as they spread across the page. Plus, you can decorate the envelope any way you like and choose a stamp that means something to you. I've received beautiful letters and envelopes from her. They always make my day and send me smiling into the world. I'm not as artistic as she is, but I try, and she says that she loves them. But, of course, she would say that.

I remember one envelope in particular. On the outside of the back flap she'd carefully printed these words in green ink, 'the essence of every wisdom is alive in the universe'. On the rest of the envelope there were hundreds of tiny flowers in all different colors. In the center of some of the flowers there were small letters, but I couldn't make them spell anything. It must have taken her hours to do. It was a masterpiece. I wondered if it caught the eye of the people in the post office. I wondered if they would want to receive an envelope like this, something so special. Did they also wonder what was inside, since the outside was so beautiful?

It had been a challenging year for me. Before I met Little Buddha, I had stayed on the surface of my life, pretty much floating along without any real direction. But she showed me what was underneath and it was what I discovered there that changed me. I couldn't go back. I wouldn't go back. Everything I experienced now, I knew there was more to it. That was especially true of my feelings. I had always thought that life was about 'thinking'. That's certainly how I was brought up. Those who did well in school seemed to me to be rewarded, while those that didn't, were told to try harder. There seemed to be a premium placed on the intellect. But Little Buddha often asked me, "So how do you feel about that?", whenever we were talking about something. I finally asked her, "Why do you always ask me that?". I had never really focused any attention on my feelings.

She told me that 'feelings' are what are most important. They are what connects you to your divine self and to the universe. It had taken me a long time to see what she meant. One of the things that helped me the most was when I followed a suggestion that I heard our minister say. He recommended spending time with my feelings. To go beyond what I 'thought' and see what would happen if, at least for part of the day, I wrote about how I 'felt'. It is a practice that I love. I've been doing it now for over a year, 561 days to be exact. I've promised myself that on each anniversary I'll reread my 'feelings journal' for the prior year's entries and then sit back and 'feel' what they mean to me. The first year was awesome. So many insights. I now understand why she places so much value on feelings.

In one of my letters to her I told her about some of what it was like for me growing up and how that shaped my life. I tried to explain where all of my beliefs came from but I couldn't. Everyone always says to me that it all goes back to your parents, but that's not true, at least not in my case. I know a lot of it was school and some was from church, two places that I assumed would help me. But as I felt my way through things, it didn't seem that school or church had helped me. I told her that I never knew that I was allowed to ask for things. In fact, quite the opposite. The words I so often heard were, "you're on your own", and I was given the distinct impression I had to 'earn' everything. In church, I was told that 'grace' was a gift, but only for a chosen few. It was for special and deserving people. No one ever told me that I fell into that category. I was told that I could ask for things, but I could not 'expect' to receive them. And further, that the granting of these requests was 'conditional', but I never knew what the conditions were. I was asked, "Do you think that you are a good person?" This led to the constant need to 'justify' that I 'deserved' whatever I was asking for. And if I ever got to thinking I was worthy, others would always find flaws in my thinking or in my actions. I was asked, "Who do you think you are to merit such special attention?" After a while I stopped asking for anything. It seemed easier. I realized that I had absorbed this worldly pattern into my everyday 'inside' life. No one on the outside had to limit me anymore or question me about what I deserved because I was doing that to myself. I had placed conditions on what I deserved, conditions I knew I could not meet. I imagined she would have a lot to say about all of this when we were next together.

The next letter I received from her was in a plain white envelope with block letters that spelled out my name and address. It was a shock. I wasn't sure that I wanted to open it. Was she that upset with me? Had I let her down? Was she tired of me expressing my challenges? I admit that, I waited several days before I got up the courage to look inside. And then I received another even bigger shock, there was only one small piece of paper in the envelope. I pulled it out and focused on it. There were only three words, 'come see me'.

It was interesting that this was just before my summer vacation, when once again I'd be going to the beach and would be able to spend time with her. I wondered the whole time what she was going to say to me. Part of me felt blank and empty, just like her envelope.

I'm here now and I'm rounding the corner and heading up her alleyway to the ocean. I hear her before I see her. Her golden voice is singing a tune I don't recognize. I wonder, how is it possible that anyone could sound so angelic, so ethereal? I stop so I can listen and feel. So magnificent!

Suddenly she stopped singing. "You might as well come in Sam", I hear her say.

I knew it shouldn't still surprise me, after all this time, but I could not understand how she knew when I was about to arrive. She could not possibly have seen me, and yet she knew.

Oh, what difference did it make? It just unnerved me somehow.

"Hi, Claire," I said, as I came through the gate to her yard. She ran to me and threw her arms around me. It was like being embraced by heaven. I didn't know why, but I started to cry. They were happy tears because I was home again. She leaned back from me and looked up into my glistening eyes.

She smiled and said, "So I guess you're happy to see me, huh?"

What an understatement.

"Well come in, we have lots to discuss," she said as she led me over to our familiar lawn chairs.

"Yes," I respond, "and let's start with the unrewarding letter you sent me. Did you lose your crayons or something? Talk about a plain and boring envelope!"

"I wanted your full attention and I thought that might do it," she grinned at me. "I guess it worked. Do you know why I sent it the way I did?', she asked, still grinning.

"Not really. Am I going to have to guess or are you going to tell me? No wait," I said, "I think I know the answer to that. Of course, I'm going to have to work for it, right?" I watched her grin increase even more. I knew it. "Okay, I suppose the blank envelope is your way of reminding me that the way I'm looking at my life is too plain. That I'm missing all of the beauty beneath the surface, like the absence of all of your beautiful designs on the envelope." I guess the way I said it, it was more a question than a statement.

"Good try," she said, "really good try, but not what I intended. That's why I included the message, 'come see me'. That was the message. If I spent time embellishing the outside of the envelope it would have taken longer for you to get here and I wanted to see you, sooner, rather than later."

"That's all? That's what it meant? Why didn't you just call me on the phone if you wanted me to get here sooner? Why wait for the mail to reach me?" I was really confused.

"Oh Sam," she said, "as much as I love you, it's not just about you." She continued, "You see I wanted to arouse the curiosity of your letter carrier. Right at this moment she's wondering why there was no magic on the outside of that envelope."

Don't ask me how, but I knew that Little Buddha was right. Somehow, she was interacting with June, my letter carrier. You see, I still didn't see all the connections. June is another 'dot' to Little Buddha. Another part of the divine chain.

"So, who are you designing the envelopes for, me or June?" I had to ask. I admit I was a little miffed.

"Oh Sam, you still think in terms of either/or. It's never like that. It's always 'both'. Both you and June received mail from me. You, the inside and her, the outside. Did you ever notice the letters inside the flowers?"

"Yes," I said, "on one of them I did."

"Sam, they were on every letter that I sent to you. They were in a code that June would recognize. She's been working it out the whole time and having a lot of fun. She looks forward to them even more than you do."

I never would have imagined Claire doing that but now that I knew, I wasn't the least bit surprised. Why make one person happy, when you can make two people happy?"

"And I have another question for you. What do you make of the disparity between why you thought I sent the letter and why I actually did send the letter?"

Her face was serious now, all traces of her grin had vanished.

"I guess we all interpret things in our own ways," I said, hoping this was the right answer.

"Do you mean to say that we all 'assume' things in our own way?" she asked, with what seemed to me to be a little edge in her voice.

Whenever I heard that tone I stepped back. I mean I actually stepped back away from her, which in this case meant moving my chair back. It always took me by surprise. It disturbed my mental picture of her as angelic. It kind of shook me. Why was that? The answer came pretty quickly. I expected her to always be kind and patient because she loved me. Okay, I got it. 'Expecting and 'assuming' must be 'relatives' and unwelcomed relatives at that. I was catching on.

Little Buddha Book One

"Okay, sorry, by now I should...umm, I mean, it would benefit me to stop making assumptions. Instead, I would benefit from 'talking' with you or asking you what you meant. And it also would benefit me to release expectations and let you be you. If I feel I need something from you, I could just ask." That seemed to me to cover her question, but when I looked at her I knew there was more. Fortunately, it started to rain and we ran to the screened porch and got inside just before the real downpour began.

As we sat, she looked over at me. 'Gazed' would be a better word. A familiar feeling came over me. My breathing quieted, my body relaxed into my chair, my eyes closed all by themselves and an incredible calm washed over me. I heard words inside my head, she's doing that thing again, but I couldn't give them voice. They just wouldn't come out. But they didn't need to. I was being covered with love. I've never been able to describe how wonderful this feels. I was so peaceful and it seemed like I was aware of everything. It was all in such sharp focus. Suddenly, I saw a bug crawling toward me. Something about it broke my 'spell'. I looked around for something to swat it with. I reached over and grabbed a folded newspaper from the table. That would work I thought. As I raised the paper up and began to bring it down I felt Little Buddha's hand catch my arm. She stopped me in mid motion. She was so strong and held my arm so firmly. I couldn't believe she had that much strength. It was amazing.

"No Sam, we don't kill bugs. They are not our enemies. They are as sacred as you and me. They are here to live out their lives, just like you and me."

There was a special look of kindness in her eyes, both for me and for the bug. "So, what do you do?", I asked.

She said, "Watch and I'll show you." She came back carrying a small box with two words written on one side, BUG BOX. Under these letters, there were a series of marks, grouped in fives. I quickly counted forty-four of them.

She went over to where the bug was crawling and carefully held the box on the floor just in front of it. With her other hand, she gently nudged the bug into the opening until it walked inside. Then she tipped the box up and closed the flaps. When her passenger was secure, she walked outside and laid the box on the ground and opened the flaps. Out came the bug, free again. Her forty-fifth rescue.

I was staring at her through the screen. What divine love she possessed, to care for such an insignificant creature. As soon as I said the words to myself I knew they were wrong. There was nothing insignificant about this bug. I share its creator, and I am a part of the same creation. And I was going to thoughtlessly kill it. I probably wouldn't have even given it a second thought. So how did I feel now? That might take me a minute.

Little Buddha looked at me as she came back inside and sat down. She had a serene look on her face. I knew she knew so many things about how life really worked, how it was all connected, how even one small bug mattered.

"Sam, let's talk about your letter now. I want to ask you something, but I don't want you to answer right away. I want you to sit with it overnight, then come back tomorrow so we can talk more about it." She paused for a few seconds then said, "How are the thoughts you shared in your letter like that small bug?"

I don't know what I thought she was going to ask me, but that sure wasn't it. I repeated the question to myself, how are the thoughts I shared in my letter like that small bug? I thought, it might take me more than one night to get this right.

"Sam, I have to stop you. There is no 'right' answer. There is only 'your' answer."

Again! Again, she was reading my mind. How did she do that? Why did she do that? I was about to ask but realized she'd said something really important to me. So, I sat still and slowed my breathing. It was an awesome observation on her part. It was true, I was still searching for the 'right' answer. It was my way of feeling rewarded. It was like food to me, a kind of addiction. It started me thinking. What had I told her in the letter? I tried to sum it up in my mind. Let's see; intellect rewarded, not allowed to ask, that I was on my own, and that I had to earn everything. Oh, and there was more. 'Grace' only applied to the deserving few and I was on the outside looking in on that one. And that absence of grace seemed to connect to my not expecting anything and that everything was conditional and that I had limits, first from those on the outside, then from myself on the inside. No wonder she asked me about the letter. No wonder she wanted me to 'come see her'. Okay, I got that these weren't

Little Buddha Book One

very upbeat things to think, but what did that have to do with that small bug? What had she said when she stopped me from killing the bug? Oh yes, she said that 'bugs are not our enemies, they are sacred and they are here to live out their lives, just like me'.

"Do you need a clue?", she asked.

"Of course," I said, "I always seem to need a clue to answer your questions. What have you got for me?"

"The answer you are seeking is from your heart, not from your head."

Well I had all night to think about it, and I wanted to get started. She must have known because she got up and hugged me goodbye.

"See you tomorrow, sunshine," she said, "Sweet dreams."

I loved it when she called me 'sunshine'. "Yes, sweet dreams to you too Claire."

So now here I am in my cottage sitting with her question. I have a beautiful view of the water and can see the luminous edge of the waves in the moonlight as they crash on shore. The sound is one of my favorite things in this world, so soothing to my spirit. It's like listening to the heart beat of the ocean.

I'm waiting for some kind of answer to appear. And here it comes. My thoughts are not my enemies, even if they appear to be. I can do as she had done. I can gently hold each one of them and then 'take them outside' and let them go. I remember picking up the newspaper to kill the bug. It reminded me of how I try to deal with my thoughts. I try to kill them, but it never works. Actually, it seems to make them stronger. How beautiful it would be if I took the gentle approach and carefully nudged them into my own 'bug box' and then took them outside and let them go. That felt really good to me.

She'd said something else, she'd said that each bug is sacred. Could it be that each of my thoughts were sacred? Could I make that make sense to me? She said the key was my heart, not my head. That's good because my head didn't see any connection. So, I went inside, just like I do when I write in my feelings journal and I asked my heart, how do I feel about this?

Little by little a feeling grew. Every thought is sacred because it leads me through my life. It connects one moment to the next. It offers me meaning and a choice. I can accept the thought or gently release it. I am not a prisoner of any one thought. If it feels of no benefit to me, I can let it go. The weightlessness of this feeling was beautiful.

Little Buddha had also said that the bug was here to live out its life, just like I was. What was the parallel here? That we were each a part of creation, deserving our own opportunity to experience our chosen life? I wasn't sure this was what she meant, but it felt true to me.

The next morning, the sun was out, the breeze was sweet and fresh and had that unmistakable ocean smell that makes me glad I am alive.

I tried to sneak up on her. I thought that if I was really quiet, maybe she wouldn't hear me. I was almost at her gate when I heard her voice.

"Nice try my friend, but I heard you a mile away." She was giggling and it was infectious. I couldn't help it and I started to laugh too. Maybe next time.

Little Buddha Book One

She asked me how I was. "I feel wonderful today, thank you. How about you?" I knew what she was going to say before she said it, but I still wanted to hear it.

"I feel divine," she said. "How did it go last night...any bugs?"

"Very funny," I responded. And then I told her everything that came to me. I watched her face to see what her reaction was. I was rewarded with an amazing smile. I couldn't imagine that god's smile is any sweeter or more beautiful.

She looked at me and said, "I love what you felt, what you expressed. I thank you for going inside to see that there is more to life than just the surface. There's one more thing about your letter I'd like to tell you. Every one of the thoughts you wrote speaks of 'limit'. I want you to know, to feel what is real. There are no limits. Every single thing is possible. It is your choice what to believe, but I tell you, you are a sacred being, a part of the whole, connected to everything, limitless."

She came over to me and placed her arms around me and in her hug, I felt the truth.

Little Buddha Book One

the room

Little Buddha Book One

the room

It was another sunny day and we headed for the beach. We could hear the waves crashing in the distance. We both carried boogie boards and discussed how to catch a wave and ride it all the way to shore. I've loved boogie boarding since I was a little boy. It still thrilled me.

When we got closer, Little Buddha kicked off her sandals and started running and yelled back at me, "Race you." What a little cheater!

I did manage to catch up and get ahead, but then tripped and fell onto the beach in a heap. While I lay there, I could hear her triumphant voice yelling, "I won!" It was nice to see this part of her, this wise wonderful being, was still a little kid at heart.

She splashed out into the water, paddling furiously and in minutes was up riding a gorgeous wave. I had just managed to get back up in time to see her ecstatic face as she balanced her way to shore.

"Well thank you for checking to see if I was okay," I said, mostly laughing.

"You're welcome," she responded, adding, "did you have a nice fall?"

"I guess sympathy isn't one of your strong suits, is it?"

She dropped her board and came over and brushed some sand off my knees. "You look pretty okay to me," she said. "Were you expecting to get hurt?"

Hmmm, was I expecting to get hurt? Well no, not really, but who would have, considering I wasn't thinking I was going to fall in the first place. Was there more to her question? There had to be, there always was, but I couldn't think of what it could be. It just seemed to me that she could have been more concerned about me. I decided to drop it.

We spent almost three hours boogie boarding. It was fantastic. One of those unforgettable days. We had to admit though we were really hungry, so we decided to walk back to her cottage for lunch.

Little Buddha's mom, Janine, had gone to town to do some shopping so we had the kitchen to ourselves. Once lunch was ready we sat at the dining room table. There were hundreds of

Little Buddha Book One

small rainbows gliding across the room, landing everywhere. I looked at her front window. There must have been over forty prisms hanging there. It was pure magic. I thought to myself, how wonderful it would be if everyone could live, surrounded by such magnificence.

"When I'm gone, do you think it will be as beautiful as it is here?", I asked.

"I guess that depends on where you are going," she answered.

"You know what I mean, when I'm dead, will it be beautiful where I go?"

Her answer totally surprised me.

"It will be as you choose it to be. What do you want to experience when you die?"

"I'm not sure what I want, but what difference does that make? Isn't it already set up by god?"

She looked at me. Her eyes were bright and alive. Her little lop-sided grin opened up into a full radiant smile. I wondered, what is up with her today?

71

"Sam, despite all of our conversations, you still don't get it, do you? God wants what you want. You have free will to choose anything you can imagine and it can all be as you see it. If you want rainbows, you can have rainbows."

I know we've talked about a lot of things and my world has expanded enormously, but this feels like too much. Did she just say that god wants what I want? How can that be? I've always been told that I was supposed to do what god wanted, not the other way around. Actually, what I've been told is that I am required to do what god wants, or else something 'bad' would happen to me and here is this young girl, the wisest person I've ever known, rocking my world. Does she expect me to truly believe I can have things the way I want, both now and once I'm in heaven?

"Claire, I know that you know a lot more than I do, probably more than I'll ever know, but seriously, what are you telling me?" I needed to hear more. I needed clarification.

"Sam, I'm sorry you've been told harmful things and suffered needlessly. I want you to know that god's greatest gift to each one of us is 'free will'. The freedom and ability to choose anything we want without expectation, requirement, obligation or repercussion." Little Buddha eyed me carefully and held my gaze with her eyes. "This is really important, Sam. Do you understand what I'm saying?"

"I think I understand what you're saying, I'm just not sure I believe what you're saying." I had to be honest with her. I owed her that.

"I thought there were 'rules'. You know, 'laws', which we have to obey. But if I can do what I want and that's what god wants, wouldn't I be able to break all of the rules?"

"Sam, just because your free will gives you the ability to choose to 'break the rules', doesn't mean that you have to. You may appreciate the value of the rules and choose to abide by them. What I'm saying is that god gives you the choice. You can live your life free to make any decision you want. God never says 'no', so when you choose, god is with you and behind you."

It seemed to me that she had a hopeful expression on her face as she watched me, like maybe I would finally get it.

I looked at her. "You know me. You know I need examples to truly understand what you're telling me. I could really use one right now." I felt like I was begging more than asking, but I was okay with that. I wanted desperately to know what she meant This whole idea confused me. Was god really going to allow me to choose my own way? And whatever way I chose would be okay with god? I was glad to see she was about to start her story.

"Okay," she said. "There was a girl, about fourteen, who awoke one day in a small hut with a grass roof and dirt floor. She was lying on a bed that faced the door. It was morning and she could see the sunshine as it slanted bright rays through openings in the hut walls. She got up, lifting the flap covering the door and walked outside. She followed a path leading away from the hut and next to a small creek. It was pleasantly warm, and she was clothed in a simple yellow knee length dress. The path crossed the creek over a wooden bridge. The air smelled sweet, and she could hear birds singing in the distance. In front of her there was a large round building. She walked around it and found there was only one door. She opened it and went inside. The room was empty except for one chair in the middle of the room. She walked over to it and sat down. It was soft and very comfortable. It had two cushioned arms and a high back. On one arm, there was a square box with a toggle switch sticking up, like the 'joy stick' on the video games she used to play. She touched it and was able to move it forward and backward and from side to side. In fact, she could move it a full 360 degrees. She found that the chair also swiveled in a full circle. What was this place for? How odd, she thought. It made her think to herself and remember the last time she was baffled like this. It had been when a man had unexpectedly given her a present. She didn't even know him. Why would he do that?

As soon as she recalled the gift and the person who had given it to her, the image of the event came to life all around her. What she'd believed was a plain wall was now alive with the exact image in her mind. She could see every single detail. At first, she was only focused in front of her, but as she swiveled in the chair, she could see the image completely encircling her. This was awesome!

As she continued turning, her hand bumped the joy stick and the scene jumped forward in time. Wow, what was happening?

As she watched, she realized that she was seeing everything and everyone who was a part of that event. She saw the man come toward her with the present in his hand. She watched him extend his arm and offer it to her. As she took the present, she could sense the weight of it and hear his words, "This is for you." She could feel the same warm, confusing, wonderful feelings as if it were happening all over again. It was beautiful and mysterious and there was something beyond her own feelings that she sensed.

She'd been wondering ever since she bumped the joy stick, why it was there and what did it do? She reached down and gently moved it in the direction of the man. The picture shifted and the view now was from his perspective. She was now looking out of his eyes, at herself holding the present. This was incredible. She was inundated with new feelings. There was a sense of apprehension, but it gave way to curiosity and then joy. There was a profound sense of love spiraling around inside of her and a feeling of true happiness. What was this all about? How could she be feeling all these things? And then it dawned on her. It was as if she were inside the man, feeling everything he felt. She was looking through his eyes, seeing her own face on the screen, watching her expressions change from anxiousness to surprise then acceptance and happiness. It was such a beautiful exchange, so simple, yet so deep.

She sat for quite a while absorbing the whole scene, able to notice even the smallest of details. There was a chemistry between them, something tangible. She knew what it was. They were sharing 'love'.

She moved the joy stick toward her image on the screen. She felt a shift, a familiarity, a return to her own senses. She moved the stick forward and watched as she opened the present. Inside was a very colorful box with a letter "A" on it. How could he have known her name was Alexandra. She lifted the lid, revealing purple tissue paper. She carefully peeled it back and saw an intricately carved butterfly. It was spectacular, so detailed, almost as if it were alive. Did he know that butterflies were her favorite? How could he? Who was he?

She felt confused and overwhelmed. She pushed the joy stick forward again and heard her words, "Thank you. What does this mean? Who are you? Why have you given this to me?"

She knew what to do next. She moved the stick forward and heard his response, "It is a present for you. I have accepted my own challenge. A challenge to perform intentional acts of kindness in this world. You are my very first act. That's why your box has a letter "A" on it. I don't know you, but I love you, because you are a part of me, just as everyone here on earth is. I chose a butterfly for my first gift because I am emerging out of my own cocoon, into a new life. I would love to give everyone a present. I would love to share joy and spread happiness to the whole world."

She moved the joy stick toward him and knew he spoke the truth. She could feel his heart expand and sensed his loving generous spirit.

She thought about what he said and what she had assumed. She believed he chose the letter "A" because of her name and the butterfly as a gift because it was her favorite. And now she knew he had very different reasons for choosing as he did. She sat and asked herself, do I make assumptions like these about everything in my life? What am I missing because I assume I know? Would it change my world if I asked instead of believing I already know?

After a while the girl leaned forward in the chair, and wondered, what would it feel like to relive her whole life like this? What revelations would there be? What changes would she make? She decided she would come back here again one day.

Claire was looking at me, waiting for me to say something.

"That was an awesome story, truly awesome. I get it. It would change everything if you could see what impact you were having on others." I started to cry. I didn't even feel it coming. It just burst out of me in a torrential downpour. I couldn't even identify all of the emotions.

I sat staring out the window for a long time. Finally, I felt the calm returning. "Claire, that was really incredible, but please forgive me, I still don't understand. What does the story have to do with free will and god wanting what I want?"

"I could just tell you, but I think it would be a lot more rewarding if you see it for yourself. I have another project for you."

"Of course, you do," I said, "whenever you get that look, I know there is going to be more work for me. What do you have in mind this time?"

"Sam, I'd like you to perform twenty acts of intentional kindness this coming week. They can be any size you want and for anyone you want. I'd like you to keep a journal that tells about them. I'd like you to focus on how you feel, before, during and after each one of them." She picked up a book off the table and handed it to me. "Here you go," she said.

Of course, it was a brand-new journal ready to be filled with observations. How could she have known our conversation would lead to this? No matter how long I spent with her, she constantly surprised me.

I have to admit it, the idea really appealed to me. I wondered though why the use of the word 'intentional', rather than what I was familiar with as 'random acts of kindness'? I guess it made sense, there wasn't anything 'random' about what I was going to do. Mine would be planned. Would that make a difference? I guess I'd find out.

A plan was already forming in my head, as I walked out into her yard. "Claire, does this mean I can't see you for a week?"

"You should be so lucky," she responded, giggling and pushing me playfully out the gate. "I'll always want to see you, Sam. How about tomorrow?"

"Count on it," I said.

I had an interesting time coming up with ideas for things to do. Some of them were simple, like holding the door open for someone or putting a stray shopping cart away. Others took a bit of planning. One day I bought two dozen carnations and handed them out to strangers on a busy downtown sidewalk. Their reactions were interesting and wide ranging. I could tell that some of them were guarded, giving me the impression they felt I had some ulterior motives. But there were folks who seemed genuinely happy, as if I'd made their day. A few actually said that to me. It prompted me to consider again why I was doing this. Was it because I wanted or expected some kindness in return?

I also found it curious that many of my intentional acts meant I would not see any reaction from the recipients. This was because I left money in various places for people to find and use, if they needed it, like the laundromat or the photocopier at the library. I felt disconnected and wondered what they thought or felt about this anonymous gift.

For this process, I decided that I would spend a certain amount of money, but found that I far exceeded it. I discovered that didn't trouble me at all. I was happy to do it. I bought ice cream for a couple, gave balloons to sick children, dropped off flowers at the nursing home and left a huge tip for a waitress, as much as the whole meal cost. I kind of wanted to stick around and see her face, but I didn't.

Not all of the acts cost money. One day I promised myself that my gift would be to fully and completely listen to each person I met. I'd never realized how much time I'd spent thinking about the next thing I wanted to say, while they were talking. It was really difficult to just listen, but so rewarding, at least it felt that way to me.

When I was recording my observations in my journal I noted, that despite my intention of wanting to give freely, I experienced a variety of other thoughts and emotions. At times, I had expectations of some kind of reciprocation. Other times I actually felt I was giving out of a sense of obligation or for some personal validation that I was a good person. Once I even felt that I was trying to manipulate a situation in order to get what I wanted. All of these feelings were unwanted and actually, unwelcomed. As I continued to perform my intentional acts, I felt a wonderful shift inside. I recognized that it really wasn't about what I was 'doing' so much as what I was 'feeling'. The more I got in touch with this, the deeper it went, and I began giving from my heart and not my head. Kindness seemed to overflow from me. It was an awesome feeling. I decided I wanted to continue this practice beyond my commitment of twenty, perhaps even for the rest of my life.

It's been a week. We sat together and she calmly waited for me to start the conversation. After another minute, I launched in, and told her everything I could remember. She asked me a lot of questions. Most of them made me think really hard, but it was so worth it. Toward the end of our conversation I said to her, "Claire, thank you so much for suggesting this to me. It was fascinating and so rewarding, especially once I realized that when I engage my heart everything lit up. It was beautiful." Claire closed her eyes and deepened her breathing. I thought she might want to rest in silence for a while, but instead she asked me another question.

"Imagine that someday you will be offered the opportunity to relive your entire life, experiencing not only your thoughts and feelings but those of everyone else that you interact with. What do you think your response would be?"

It was a mind-boggling thought. Actually, I wasn't sure if I'd say 'yes' or 'no'. Then I recalled how it felt when in the story, the girl shared the feeling of love with the man, when she received his present. Yes, I did want that. I would risk some possible negative experiences, if I could feel that kind of love as well.

Claire interrupted my thoughts. "Do you see that performing intentional acts of kindness is an expression of your free will? No one made you do this. I suggested it, but you chose it, just as the man did in the story. And you discovered that not all reactions were the same and the reason for this is that everyone exercised their own free will in responding. They chose their own path, not the one you wanted or perhaps expected."

She smiled at me and waited to see if I wanted to respond. I didn't, so she continued, "Sam, imagine for a moment that you are god, what do you want?"

Talk about a hard question to answer. "I don't know," I said, "Is that really something anyone can answer?"

"Sam, there isn't a right or wrong answer, I just want to see what your sense is. Just say the first thing that comes to you, okay?"

"Well, I would want everyone to be happy and live in peace, I'd want everyone to be able to do what they wanted, as long as they didn't hurt others."

"See, that wasn't so hard," she responded. "What do you think you would do if people did hurt each other? Would you punish them? And for that matter, if they didn't hurt others, but always showed love and compassion, would you reward them?"

I think I was beginning to see how things might work. If she was right and that god had given each of us 'free will', the ability to make choices about everything in our lives, then how could I reward or punish their actions? They were just using the gift I had given them. Otherwise, wasn't I making them all puppets, doing only what I told them? I'd never thought about this before, but it made a lot of sense to me.

"Claire, are you saying that because god gave us all free will to make any choice we wish, that god wants what we want, what we're choosing in each moment?"

Her answer was a simple, "Yes".

"You see Sam, each of us is a part of god, each able to choose our own path. If it is our desire to experience fear and a feeling of separation, we know inside ourselves what choices to make and if we want to experience love and unity, we also know deep inside, what choices will bring this into our lives. Free will is the gift you choose with."

She could see the wheels spinning in my mind. "Sam, there is so much more for us to talk about. It's more beautiful than you can currently imagine. Let's sit with this for now. I promise we'll come back to this later, okay?"

It was more than okay.

a million of you

Little Buddha Book One

a million of you

I was holding the two pieces of wood firmly together as she hammered in several nails. We'd been at this for a while now, and it was starting to look pretty good to me. After a few more nails, she stood back to admire her work.

"I think it needs some bracing and then it will be done," she said. "I hope I measured everything correctly."

She attached some right-angle braces and secured them in place. "That's it," she said, "we're all set."

We stood the bookshelf upright. It was beautiful, solid oak and covered with a rich dark stain.

She started transferring the heavy books from the floor, setting them in place one by one. I had to hold them so they wouldn't fall over, until they spanned the full width of the shelf. There were thirty volumes in total, with different letters printed on their spines.

"So," I said, "this is the famous Encyclopedia Britannica I've always heard about."

"Yes, isn't it gorgeous? I love the way the books feel so…'substantial'. Maybe it's because of all the knowledge inside of them. Did you know there are 32,640 pages that make up this set?"

"I had no idea there were that many. How do you know that's the correct count?" She was always astounding me with the trivia she knew. I thought maybe this time she was kidding me.

"Sam, did you know that, since I was little, my mom has been homeschooling me?"

I hadn't known. It never came up before.

"One of our projects was to read the whole encyclopedia from cover to cover. It took us over two years. It was absolutely fascinating. I think it would benefit me to read it all again, because this edition was printed in 1974. It's on-line now of course, so I've already started to see what's new."

I couldn't imagine reading thirty volumes cover to cover. The longest book I'd ever read was maybe six hundred pages. It's incredible what she must know. "Do you feel pretty smart?", I asked.

"The things I learned are just a foundation. They represent what some people think is the truth. It's curious, but a lot of what it says, people now see differently. Facts don't always stay as facts. And so too, the truth appears to change depending on who you are talking with."

She looked a bit pensive, I thought. "Okay then, so how do we ever know what the truth is?", I asked, genuinely interested.

"You can only know your own truth," she responded.

I could feel a change in direction coming. She did this to me all the time. A moment ago, I thought there was probably one truth. But now I'm wondering. She just said, you can only know your OWN truth. What could that possibly mean? Could everyone on earth have their own truth? She was looking at me. There appeared to be a question in her eyes. "What?" I asked.

"Tell me something Sam," she said, "what is one thing you know to be true? Something that doesn't have more than one answer. Something everyone agrees with."

Oh, brother! I started an inventory in my mind. "How about gravity?" I thought that was a good place to start. Didn't everything eventually fall down?

"Gravity where?", she responded, "here or in space?"

Hmmm, I forgot about space. I suggested a few more ideas, you have to eat to stay alive, diamonds are the hardest substance, one plus one is two. She countered each and every suggestion I made. After a while I wondered, did it really matter that there weren't any absolutes?

She smiled and started to giggle a little. Clearly, she found me amusing. "I have another question for you Sam."

"One I can answer?" I hoped.

"Maybe. Imagine anything. What's the first thing that comes to your mind?"

"A candy bar," I told her. It helped that I was holding one at the moment.

"Okay, can you tell me how it was made?" Her smile was getting bigger now.

"Not really", I answered. I mean I know there is chocolate and caramel in it. It's covered with a wrapper, but that's about it I guess." I was wondering where she was going with all of these questions and answers Was she trying to prove how little I really knew?

"Sam, there's one thing I learned while reading the encyclopedia. It's that we really don't KNOW much of anything. I'd bet that very few people could tell you how ANYTHING is made. I mean the whole process, where the ingredients come from, how they're transported along their path, who makes them, how did the people who made them learn their skill, what does the product do for us or do to us. There are hundreds of questions we can't answer. It's amazing really if you stop and think about it. Even something as simple as the life cycle of a blade of grass. And then there's US. Who are we? Why are we here? How many 'states' are we made of; emotional, mental, physical, spiritual? What connects us?" She stopped for a moment, her head moving slowly from side to side.

Wow! I was feeling a bit overwhelmed. In the space of a few minutes we'd gone from building a book shelf to here. And where was 'here'? "Okay, I admit it, I don't really know much of anything. Not outside myself and probably not inside myself," I said.

She could see by my expression that I was losing it. "Sam," she said, "do you want the 'good news'?"

"Absolutely," I responded, "all that you can give me."

"Now you're really ready to learn!" Her eyes met mine.

The dizziness I was feeling subsided and something approaching calm took hold of me. I started breathing slower and deeper. I closed my eyes and let go, dropping back into the ocean of myself. "I'm not sure I understand what you mean, that now I'm really ready to learn?"

"The biggest barrier to learning anything is thinking you already know everything about it." She gave me one of those dazzling smiles of hers. "I have a suggestion for you. A project to try. Are you interested?"

Her projects were challenging, but they were always worth my effort. "Yes, I'm ready. What did you have in mind?"

"I'd like you to spend a week observing a tree and then tell me what your observations are. Start today. Pick just one tree and see what happens. Okay?"

"Yes," I said, "I'll give it a try."

On my way back to my cottage, I saw a lot of trees, certainly more than I'd noticed before. I was surprised to see that they came in so many sizes. And their bark and leaves and needles were all different. So were their colors. It was going to be hard to choose just one.

I continue walking. I noticed that not only the trees, but the shrubs and flowers and stones along the path were all unique. Was this possible? Why hadn't I ever realized this before? Something caught in my mind. I had known this before. It was when I was a very small boy. I used to pretend that I was an ant and I would lie on the ground for a long time looking carefully at everything within reach. I could do that for hours. I understood that was what Little Buddha was asking me to do again. I was getting excited now for my new project. Just as I was thinking about this, I spotted the tree I wanted to observe. It was a huge oak tree in the middle of a cemetery. I decided I'd come back first thing in the morning with my pen and notebook.

I went to the cemetery the next day, and it was a beautiful sunny day. I pressed my hands against the trunk, feeling the pattern of the bark, first with my eyes open, then with them closed. I stood there for a long time. So long in fact, that I began to feel a part of the tree. I could smell its aroma, sort of sweet and nutty. I really liked it. I could feel a sensation on the back of my hands every so often. I opened my eyes and saw an ant crawling across, using my hand as a bridge. I could see further up the tree, that where there was an indentation, some moss had grown and out of it a seedling was growing. The tree, 'my' tree, was host to another tree. It might not even be another oak, but a different species altogether. That was amazing to me. All day long I observed new things, especially when I changed positions.

The next day I climbed up about twelve feet and sat in one of the main branches. There was a whole different bug colony here for me to study. After a while it was hard to stay comfortable, so I climbed back down. When I got to the ground, I noticed several acorns there. I held them in my hands. I was surprised to find they felt, I don't know, 'familiar'. I knew what it was but didn't want to acknowledge it to myself. They had the same energy, the same feeling as the rest of the tree. What did that mean?

Every day there I felt new connections to the tree and as I opened my heart, an incredible thing happened. I felt the tree 'talk' to me. I don't mean out loud of course. But I heard it inside my head like some form of telepathy, I suppose. I heard my tree tell me that it was kin to the tree across the road about thirty feet away. That they were soul mates and that their roots were intertwined. I felt like I could ask questions and get answers. Was I delusional? Every time I questioned myself, the connection faded. I didn't want that. I loved this tree and I wanted to know more. This tree had become my friend. Was that possible? I guess I was at a crossroads. Should I believe my head or my heart? What was Little Buddha always saying to me...what do you feel?

I decided to let go of my thinking. After all, what did I really KNOW about anything? Maybe that wasn't as important as what I felt. The truth for me was that I loved this tree and I knew we were connected. I felt it completely.

Little Buddha Book One

The week was over and I was headed to Claire's cottage. As I neared my tree I could feel a sense of happiness race through me. I wrapped my arms around him. That's right, my tree was a 'him'. It may sound strange, but I felt it hugged me back. I wished I'd known about trees a long time ago. It would have really helped me. But I knew now and that was what was important.

When Claire saw me, her face was expectant and I sensed her curiosity.

"So, tell me everything," she said excitedly as she led me to our favorite chairs. Her arm was looped around mine. It felt so nice to be with her.

I told her all the details I could remember. She seemed pleased but I could tell she was waiting for more. I hadn't told her about the 'conversations' I'd had with my tree yet.

"So, what else happened? Sam, I know you're holding out on me. I can see it in your eyes."

I jumped in. "You might not believe me if I tell you," I responded.

Little Buddha Book One

"Do you believe you?" she asked, with a serious expression on her face.

I considered before answering. "Yes, I do."

"Then I believe you," she said, "Please tell me."

"Well, I had several conversations with my tree and was told things I'd never imagined. My tree told me that his leaves in the fall brighten when passersby admire them. He said that sometimes they even glow when the sun hits them just right. He told me that all trees absorb the feelings of those who stand near them. My tree in the cemetery feels the pain and longing of many people. My tree told me that it exchanges energy with the world. I'd always heard about how important trees were but I'd never known that trees take in what we breathe out and, along with sunlight and water, they produce life giving oxygen for us."

There was more. "I love my tree. I feel so at peace when I'm there with him. Even now, thinking and talking about him, I feel calm and happy."

"Sam, that's wonderful. I'm so glad you decided to invest your heart in this project.

98

Sometimes we're reluctant. We've been hurt or laughed at because we've expressed our feelings. There is a sense of distrust we're taught, about moving beyond our mind. Do you remember what we were talking about last week? I'll remind you. We were talking about the 'truth'. Do you recall what I said to you?"

"I believe you said, that you can only know your own truth." I was pretty sure I had it right.

"Yes, and do you see what that means now? You spent a week observing the world. You used your own eyes. You used all of your senses. And opened your heart. You discovered for yourself and though others may not believe you, you know your own truth."

She was right. That was what happened to me. I was so much more than I had been a week ago. This meant something to me, something really important. I could do this with other things, perhaps even with people in my life. I was imagining the possibilities when I heard her voice.

"Sam, are you ready for something else, something new to you?"

Yes, I felt I was, and I told her so.

"I want to share with you what I believe about how it works here on earth. I know it's likely to move you beyond anything you've ever thought or experienced. But you know now, know it in your whole being, that there is more going on here than you ever suspected."

Well she certainly had my curiosity aroused. "What," I asked, "what do you want to tell me?"

"Sam, did you know that if you took one leaf and tore a piece off and then photographed the leaf with a special camera, the image of the torn off piece would still be visible?"

"Actually, I have heard about that," I said. "I think that's amazing."

"And are you aware that the entire blueprint for your oak tree is already present in the acorn you found?"

"Yes, I'd learned about that in school when I was young." I always found it fascinating to think about how something so small could have the inner plan to grow into something so large. "I don't remember anyone saying the design was so specific that its height or leaf pattern or root system was already determined though."

"I'm not saying it is. What I'm saying is that there is an "intention" within the acorn. But once it starts to grow, it is impacted by its environment, which affects its size and everything else," she responded.

"I see, sort of nature versus nurture for a tree, right?" I asked, thinking I knew where she was going with all of this.

"Yes," she said, "and like trees, you probably know that we human beings have a blueprint, a specific guide that governs our development."

"You're talking about DNA, right?"

"Yes. But there's more to it than our biological DNA, we each have a spiritual part of us, a general blueprint of why we came to earth and what we wish to create and experience."

"Now that I've never heard about. Is this a part of your 'truth'?"

Claire seemed very focused. It made me want to pay very close attention.

"Yes Sam. And just like the oak tree, our physical selves are affected by the environment where we live. But what I want to tell you is that our spiritual DNA has no such limits. I want you to imagine a picture in your mind. Start with one image of yourself and then two and then three and then four and keep going. Try to imagine one million images of yourself. Imagine that at any time you can be any one of these images, full and completely you. And what determines what image, is your free will. You have unlimited choices available to you."

"Wait a minute, you're going too fast for me. You're saying that at any one moment in time, that one million images of 'me' exist and that they are all forms of me, and I can choose which one to be and based on my choice, what I create or experience will be different from all other images of me?" I was a little incredulous or maybe, unnerved. Maybe both.

"Sam, I'm only using 'one million' as an example. There is no actual number because there is an unlimited number of possibilities. But yes, each one is different and unfolds in a unique way."

I was thinking hard about this. What would this mean to me? What would it mean, practically speaking? Did this open the door for me to be anything I wanted? At any time I wanted it? I had been brought up to think in terms of 'limit', that no matter what I wanted, I could only have certain things.

"Claire, what are you saying to me? Are you telling me that I am truly limitless? That I can create or experience anything I choose?"

"Yes, it is a part of who you are, who everyone is. I know you've been told otherwise. This is a chance for you to realize you don't have to accept those limited beliefs. No one does."

"That sounds wonderful, I but how do I do it? I mean, how do I get in touch with the other million images of me?" This seemed like the really important issue to me.

"Like all things, you look inside of yourself and find your truth. Never accept what I tell you, if you can't FEEL the truth in it."

Little Buddha was quite emphatic. I could tell by her tone of voice and the look in her eyes.

"I do believe you. I could feel this as truth when you were speaking. So, suppose I'm not happy with some limiting thought or belief, what do I do about that?"

Little Buddha Book One

Claire said, "You've already done the hard part by the time you realize this because you know what you are experiencing is not what you want. Because you now know that you may create or experience anything you want, you simply conceive what you do wish, believe that you are limitless and can experience anything you choose and then take action. This is the formula to create or experience anything you desire. Remember, god wants what you want and you have the free will to choose without any limits, except those you accept."

This was awesome, but I was going to have to try this out a few times to make sure it really worked. "Thank you, Claire," I said, "for sharing your truth with me. I am so grateful for you."

"It is my pleasure Sam. Now I have an idea. Let's go hug a tree."

"I know just the one," I said.

Little Buddha Book One

outside inside

Little Buddha Book One

outside inside

We were on our way back to the beach. It was a gorgeous summer day, just the right temperature, with a cooling shore breeze. It has finally occurred to me that in all the time I've known Little Buddha I've never heard her volunteer anything about herself. It seemed that she was always answering my questions or telling me a story to help me understand her point about something important to me.

"You know Claire, I'd love to know something more about you."

She turned toward me with a curious look on her face.

"What?", I asked.

"Is there something specific you'd like to know?", she responded. "I'd be happy to tell you anything. You only need to ask."

Strangely, I wasn't ready for her to be that open. She was such a mystery to me and I wanted to know more. I wanted to know everything. I decided to start small. "Well, for instance have you ever written a poem?", I asked.

"Oh yes, lots."

"What are they about? Can you read me one?" I was fascinated to think that she'd written "lots" of poems and was very curious what her subject matter would be.

"Well, the first one that comes to me is one I wrote last autumn. I went out one day to spend time with some tree friends. By the way, it's so great that you know what I mean now, about how a tree can become your friend. I'm so grateful you connected so deeply with your special tree."

I knew she was referring to one of her "assignments" to me from this summer where I observed a tree for a week. It was fantastic. I'd never look at trees again without feeling something akin to adoration. I felt I understood trees on a whole new level which was utterly amazing to me.

"So, what happened, what did you write?" I was excited to hear about her experience.

Her eyes got a little "misty" I'd say, as she spoke. "It was pure magic. I started by placing my hands on the tree trunk and closing my eyes. I have such love for trees it only takes them a few seconds to respond to me. I could hear the tree's thoughts in my head. We spent a few minutes "talking" this way before we both let go and sank into "feeling". I put my arms around her beautiful branches and leaned against her beautiful straight trunk. I felt us 'merging'. So completely delightful."

"It sounds marvelous. What else happened? I was excited to get to her poem."

"My tree knew I had a question I'd always wanted to have answered and encouraged me to ask, so I did. And that's how the poem came out." She looked off into the distance for a few seconds then recited her poem from memory.

"I went for a walk
to touch some trees

I came to one

I held my hand to its heart
I wrapped my arms around
One of its branches
And asked…

Are you sad to be losing your leaves?
And what I heard was this…

Little Buddha Book One

Are you kidding?

My beautiful halo of green leaves,
Each one a promise
Now falling yellow, orange and red,
Wishes of mine
Fulfilled

Each flying with the wind
Creating room for my new dreams

And so it is with you child,
As your heart opens
All your dreams become real."

"That was so beautiful," I said. "Thank you for sharing that with me." I savored her words while we walked. "Do you think everyone is capable of "talking" with trees?", I asked.

"Yes, unless they choose to believe it is not possible. You see, everything is possible. The only thing that ever stopped anyone from doing anything is their belief system. Some things are just too extreme for some people. Their view is so narrow it only lets in a little light, making it very difficult for them to see there is more truth in their world. But for those with wide eyes and open minds, nothing is out of their reach or experience." She stopped walking and waited for me to look at her. When my eyes met hers, she said, "Sam, do you feel bigger since your tree experience? Did you feel your whole outlook shift and expand?"

I didn't need to think about this. "Yes, very much so."

"And did it release you from some of your other limitations?"

"Yes," I said, "because once you do something you thought was previously impossible, you begin to believe other things are now within reach." I thought for a second to see if any examples would come to mind. "You know Claire, I've placed a lot of physical, mental and emotional limits on myself and I've come to realize they're not necessarily true anymore. They're only true if that's what I continue to tell myself and I realize how powerful my thought patterns are. But once you break one, it makes it a little easier to break the next. You assigning me to observing a tree for a week gave me the opportunity to open myself up. I realize that I could have stayed closed but there was much more value to being open. I want to thank you so much for that."

"You're welcome Sam," she said. "I'm wondering, do you think it is true that you are someone who likes to feel 'balance' in your life?"

"Yes, that's been really important to me. Whenever my life starts to feel challenging or unnerving, I begin to feel out of balance. Are you thinking there is a connection between my talking with my tree and my sense of balance?"

"I'm more interested in what you think about the connection or if you even think there is one."

I felt her shifting the focus back onto me and avoiding my question to her. What did I want to do about this? I could push back and try to make her answer me, but I doubted that would really work. So, I decided to see what I thought and what I felt about her question. I knew that I felt best when things in my life were in balance. I looked underneath this feeling for a minute and what came up was that I felt I needed a sense of safety and security in my life, so that's what I told her.

"Okay Sam, I get it but I'd like you to ask yourself this...what is your frame of reference?

Little Buddha Book One

What provides you with real safety and security?"

She always asked me such hard questions. Every so often I'd like a real softball. Something nice and easy to hit out of the park.

"My first reaction is that my feelings of safety are met when everything in my life is orderly. When my job is going well, I have cash in my wallet, when all of my relationships are okay and no one is fighting. And when my car isn't acting up and the fall leaves stay put until the workers come to pick them up."

Claire looked thoughtful for a moment then asked, "How many things that form the basis of your feeling of safety are under your direct control?"

"Actually, not very many of them," I responded, which was pretty disturbing to me, now that it was so obvious. I liked feeling in control. It was comfortable, but now I could see it was a false sense of security and that truly the only thing I could control was my attitude about any of these things. So, what was my frame of reference? It seemed pretty clear now. I was relying on a whole list of outside, uncontrollable events to line up before I could feel happy and in balance. It was also pretty clear to me that would never work. I needed a whole new approach. I wanted to know, was there a lesson to be learned from my tree observation experience? I released my preconceived notions about the consciousness of trees and found a new friend. If that could happen for me then what else was possible? Perhaps it was like Claire said, that anything is possible.

I told her what I'd just been thinking. She listened very carefully, as she always did, then looked into my eyes. Why did she do that? It made me realize how unusual it was in my experience and I wondered why everyone didn't do this? I wondered if I ever really looked at someone while they were speaking to me? I mean, really looked at them and paid attention. It was a change I wanted to make because I could see how invested she was in me and I loved her for this.

"Sam, do you know one of the reasons it is so hard for you to feel secure within yourself?"

I stared down at the ground then back to her, "I feel pretty sure there are lots of reasons. Did you have one in mind?"

"Yes," she said, "it's similar to something we've already talked about. Do you remember us discussing inner wisdom versus outer wisdom?"

I thought for a few seconds. "Yes, I think you made the point that I was searching outside myself for answers, and you explained that any real answers would come from inside of me. And then you pointed me toward my own truth."

"Very good."

She looked pleased 'with me' or maybe it was that she was pleased 'for me'. Either way, it felt great.

"Sam, I'm going to ask you to spend some time tonight writing down everything you can think of under two columns. Label the first one, 'inside validations' and the second one, 'outside validations', and then tomorrow we can talk."

So here I was at my familiar spot facing the ocean, watching the waves roll in. I had my two columns and my pen ready. And to myself I said, "What am I waiting for? Come on, just write these down, it can't be that hard." But it was hard, because despite how obvious maybe it should be, I couldn't think of a thing. I wondered, what is my resistance to this assignment? So, I just sat there, waiting for inspiration. Nothing.

After a while I got up and walked around and then a question hit me. Did inside versus outside mean in my head or in my heart? I'd been learning there was a really big difference between these locations. So, I decided to start there. My head began immediately with 'outside' things like job status, promotions, family success, recognition and awards, the house I lived in, the car I drove, my bank balances. I was on a roll now. But then I wondered, were there also outside validations that applied to my heart? Yes, there were. But then I wondered, was this exercise going to expand into some kind of matrix and become too complicated? I have to say I am capable of that kind of thinking. No, I wanted to keep this simple.

My next thought was perhaps it was as simple as two choices; tangible and intangible things. There were certainly physical rewards which meant something to me but there were also emotional, intellectual and spiritual rewards. Sometimes others gave me the rewards and sometimes I gave them to myself. Somehow this didn't seem to cover it.

I could hear Little Buddha in my head saying, "You're making this too hard, keep it simple." I imagined her sweet smile and relaxed. I took in a deep breath and let it out slowly. And another, and another and put my hand over my heart. Everything inside me slowed down. I remembered how much I loved this place, this feeling of love and peace inside me and there it was, so clear to me now. My answer rested right in front of me. My true frame of reference for knowing and feeling what was right for me was all about love. I knew that every point of outside validation I cared about was born of fear. Every one of them could be taken away, leaving me with nothing. I sensed that all forms of outside validation were like 'empty calories', things that tasted good at the time but did not nourish me. What I truly wanted, what sustained me and made me feel alive, all came from love. The love 'inside' of me. And the more I breathed into this love, the more it grew, until it overflowed naturally into the world. I couldn't wait to share this with Claire.

We were sitting on her patio basking in the sun. I told her everything I experienced last night and she smiled at me. I looked back at her with my own smile. I thought I could stay here for hours wrapped up in her love.

"Sam, you're doing such fine work. I'm so joyful that you are embracing your inner search and allowing yourself to find everything you need."

She got up and held her hand out to me. I took it, and she led me into her cottage, through the living room and into her art room.

"Sam, let's do a project."

I used to be afraid of her art projects but now I enjoyed them, especially if I got to use a lot of colors. "What are we going to do?", I asked.

She handed me a large sheet of white paper and a box of colored pencils. She set out the same for herself then dumped the pencils out in front of her. She drew a large sun in the middle of the paper and then rays spreading out in all directions.

"Am I supposed to do the same?" I asked.

"Yes," she said, "and then we're both going to write down all the things we can think of that truly nourish us at the end of the rays."

117

Little Buddha Book One

That sounded like fun but I wasn't sure there were that many things to write. I was wrong, as usual. Once I got started, more and more things came to me. Hers was filled in minutes.

"Show off," I teased.

"Yours is pretty full too you know!"

I thought about it. Before last summer I don't know if I could have thought of more than a couple of things. But now, my sun nourishment picture was almost full.

"I love you, Claire. Thank you so much for your wisdom and for loving me," I said, choking up a little.

Little Buddha looked over at me and held up her drawing. She raised a slender finger and pointed to the end of one of her sun rays. It was a picture of me.

My heart filled with spontaneous joy. What a wonderful way to end my summer!

118

the practice

Little Buddha Book One

the practice

The sky was absolutely clear and the air had that delicious aroma you can only find near the ocean. I walked down her alleyway to the beach on this first day of summer and heard a voice I didn't recognize coming from her cottage yard. That's interesting because I've only ever seen Little Buddha and her mom, Janine, there. It was a male voice. I wondered who it could be. I decided maybe I should knock on the gate, rather than just barge in, and so I did.

"Come in," I heard Claire's sweet voice say.

I pushed the gate open and saw a teenage boy standing with Claire and her mom. Claire ran to me and hugged me.

"How divine to see you Sam." She took my hand and led me across the yard. "I want to introduce you to my cousin, Michael. Maybe you remember my mentioning him a couple of years ago. He won't be able to hear you very well so you'll need to speak up."

He was very tall, almost my height and he had long shiny dark black hair which he wore swept away behind him so that it hung down his back. His face was smooth with no hint of a beard or moustache. His eyes were bright, and he was very handsome. He moved gracefully toward me, offering his right hand to me. I took it and said loudly, "It's wonderful to meet you Michael."

He looked me deeply in the eyes and placed his left hand on his heart and said, "I see you my brother."

I felt a beautiful wave of peace wash over me. He held my hand for a moment before letting go. I felt a little shaky, like something just happened, but wasn't sure what. He was still looking at me, a smile on his face. I felt very loved. That was the best description I have for it. I don't think I've ever met someone who I felt such an immediate connection to. It was remarkable really.

Claire broke the spell. "Sam, come and sit with us."

We all went inside and sat in the living room. Janine offered each of us a glass of iced tea and we relaxed into silence.

Again, it was Claire who spoke. "Sam, Michael's just been sharing what's been happening to him. I think you'll find it quite enlightening." She turned to Michael and nodded slightly. He seemed to understand her gesture and swiveled in his chair to face me. He was completely at ease in my presence, like we'd always known each other.

"It happened a couple of weeks ago. I'd noticed one morning that my hearing wasn't as acute as normal. The next morning, I woke up and could barely hear anything out of my left ear. Then later that day the same thing happened with my right ear." And he ended by saying, "What a remarkable gift this is to me."

"Huh?" is what I wanted to say. How could losing your hearing be considered any kind of 'gift', I thought. I'd had my share of temporary hearing issues and I found them really challenging. Each time it happened I felt disconnected from the world. Hearing was so important to me and without it my world grew infinitely smaller. And the longer it went on the worse it was for me. I didn't want to disagree with Michael or challenge him but I wanted to know how he could consider this a 'gift'.

"Sam, I can see from your expression you're confused and probably want to know why I feel the way I do," Michael said.

I should have known that since he was Claire's cousin, he could probably 'read minds' just like she could. "Yes Michael, I would," I said, relieved I wouldn't have to ask.

Michael looked down for a moment, seeming to gather his thoughts, then stared into my eyes, just like his cousin. "Sam, in my belief system everything I experience is a gift. It is something I've brought into my world to expand my awareness. The only time it ever becomes difficult is if I forget and label the experience 'bad' or 'good'. Whenever that happens it makes it very hard to remain open to the message, because I've already decided the meaning, before I've had a chance to actually see what it has to share with me." He waited to see if I wanted to respond.

I didn't. I was thinking, could someone truly live with this kind of consciousness? Because I could identify with the subject of hearing loss, I wondered if I could have ever refrained from labeling the event as 'bad'? And if I could have, could I have taken another step and waited to see what happened next? Could I have searched inside myself for some meaning, some purpose to show up? I was pondering these questions when Little Buddha prompted me with a question.

Little Buddha Book One

"Sam, I know it's important for you to think a bit more about this and I know you'll come up with great questions to consider, but please take a moment and ask yourself how you 'feel' about what Michael said." Her eyes were intense and alive and so beautiful.

"Okay," I said. "Well I feel it is a wonderful idea to be open to any experience as a gift."

"Thank you, Sam, but that is a thought not a feeling. You remember there is a very big difference, right?"

I did remember, but I also knew that my first instinct was still to think. I closed my eyes and tried to release my 'thinking mode' and relax. I became aware of my breathing, which was pretty fast, another sure sign of 'thinking'. I consciously slowed my breath and savored it moving in and out of my body. With my eyes closed I started to see colors swirling. After a few minutes, I felt very peaceful and asked myself, how did I 'feel' about what Michael said? I felt the beauty of it and the 'rightness'. It felt simple and true. It felt warm and very comforting. I kept my eyes closed and told them what I was experiencing.

124

Little Buddha Book One

"That's so good," Claire responded. "So, would you say that you 'feel' the truth, even though you still have 'thinking' questions?"

"Exactly, yes," I said. "That's a great description."

Claire asked me to open my eyes. She looked deeply into them, then turned again to Michael, who said, "Sam, it is a practice. This does not come 'naturally' to me or to any of my tribe. We get better the more we practice until some of it becomes second nature. You can learn and practice just like we do, if you want to."

"Yes, I want to," I told him. "How do I start?" It was clear he hadn't heard me, so I repeated my words a little louder. It's amazing how you can know something intellectually, like his hearing being currently impaired, and yet not remember to speak louder than normal. I suppose there was a lesson in this for me and I promised myself to consider it later.

"There are a few things that it would be helpful for you to keep in mind," he said. "The first is that nothing that happens to you in your whole life is ever 'good' or 'bad'. Each of these labels is a subjective term whose only relevance is the distance it represents from what we've

125

previously established as our 'expectation, need or desire'. I say 'previously' because every time a new experience occurs, we re-set our 'expectation, need or desire'."

I wanted to make sure I followed him and didn't get left behind by him moving to the next point too quickly. I could tell this was going to be like one of my 'conversations' with Claire. I caught the twinkle in her eyes and mischievous grin on her face and knew I was right.

"Michael," I said, "what's so wrong about labeling things 'good' and 'bad'? It does represent the way I think about it and also usually the way I feel." This seemed like a pretty key point to me and I knew I'd lose the rest of what he had to say if I didn't understand it better.

Claire looked at Michael, as if to say, can I answer this one? He blinked at her, which I guess meant, yes.

"Sam, do you remember our whole conversation about connecting the dots?", Claire said.

I did, of course. That had been huge for me.

Little Buddha Book One

"Do you remember that you labeled the loss of your job as 'bad', but later discovered how many 'good' things came out of it?"

"Yes," I said.

"Well, this is an extension of that conversation. Imagine how you would have experienced that situation if you hadn't labeled your job loss as 'bad' and all of the positive experiences that followed as 'good'?"

"What are you saying, that everything is just 'neutral?'" I was confused. I mean, I understood the intellectual idea, but in practice it seemed, without deciding if something were good or bad, the experience would be kind of meaningless.

Michael rejoined our conversation and asked me a question. "Did your job loss cause you pain or suffering?"

"Yes, a lot," I answered.

"Are you open to the idea that this is because you labeled it 'bad'? Perhaps you didn't say it out loud to yourself or others, but underneath, where you 'feel' your life, you told yourself it was a horrible thing and would require major

127

changes for you and others. Perhaps you felt your self-image was damaged or that others would think less of you. Maybe you were angry at those who made or executed the decision which led to your job loss. Does any of that feel true to you?" There was a palpable sense of sympathy in his voice and on his face.

"Yes, all of what you said is true, and more, actually." I didn't really want to admit that out loud, but I had felt all of it. "So, are you saying that all of that colored my experience in a negative way and that if I had just said to myself, this is something happening to me and I want to see what meaning this may have for me, that it would have been different?"

"That's a good start," Michael said and continued, "What I'm saying is despite the appearance that the event, your job loss, came from outside of you, it didn't. It is a part of your earth experience, something that happened which is somehow a part of your plan. I realize this represents a big shift in your belief system and of course it may take some time for you to feel its truth."

That's for sure, I thought. "So, let me see if I've got this straight. The first step is to release any need or desire to 'label' any experience or encounter."

Michael and Claire both nodded their affirmation.

"And from what you've said, the next step is to open myself to the idea that I somehow called this experience into existence?" That seemed to me what I heard Michael say. It was confusing to me because it suggested that I am in control of everything. So, I'm wondering how that is possible. How could I have 'caused' myself to lose my job? There was some danger here because I could easily see myself as an unwitting 'victim' in my own world.

Michael sat back and visibly relaxed. His facial muscles went smooth and I could hear him slow his breathing. What was fascinating to me was how much this calmed me down. "Sam, although you're right about the next step, you need a little background for it to make sense. A part of our belief system is that you have separate but integrated parts to the whole of you. You have physical, emotional, intellectual and spiritual components. These were all joined as you came into this world and took on human form. You also received an ego to help guide and navigate this earth life. Your ego is very important and helps protect you and 'keep you separate' from others, so that you can tell the difference between you and all the others present here on earth."

Michael looked at me and must have decided that I was paying attention and not lost. He said, "While you are here, your physical, emotional and intellectual parts are actively engaged and involved in everything you do, but they are not aware of your earth plan. They're sort of 'along for the spiritual ride'. Your spiritual part though, is always connected to spirit world and knows your plan, although is not always 'conscious' of it. It holds the key to your spiritual DNA, the blueprint of experiences you'd like to encounter while here on the earth plane, though none of these are set in stone."

I couldn't help interrupting, "That's because of free will, right?"

"Yes, that's right." Michael looked over at Claire who was beaming. He smiled back at her and went on speaking. "Free will gives you the constant choice to direct your life any way you'd like. You are not limited by anyone or anything. I'm sure Claire told you that god wants what you want."

I knew he wanted to continue, but I needed to interrupt again. "Yes, she did and we had a great conversation about that. I have to confess I'm still working on that though."

He smiled again at me, seemingly unfazed by my breaking in on him again. He waited a second longer to see if I was done. He was so considerate.

"Sam, it's like I said, all of this takes practice and it's not always easy to make major shifts in your beliefs, especially if there is hidden energy in them."

I believe I understood what he was saying, all except the part about 'hidden energy'. I didn't really get that, so I asked him what he meant.

"Whenever you acquire a belief and take it into your world there is an energetic component to it. Some beliefs you accept are laced with fear. You believe that if you don't accept them that you will be punished somehow or you are made to feel guilty or ashamed. These beliefs are very strong and become even stronger over time. Of course, the same is true of other beliefs that are steeped in love, but every belief you accept has something attached to it. Part of what we practice is sitting with each of our beliefs until we see what is connected to them. And then we try to release the energy so we can see the inherent value of the belief itself."

That sounded really valuable to me, but also pretty hard to practice. I wasn't sure I had the conviction it would take. "So how does this all relate to your feeling that your hearing loss is a gift to you?" I wanted to bring our conversation full circle.

"I guess the short answer is that I believe that everything that happens in my life is there to serve me, to provide meaning and wisdom and to help me remember."

Michael was watching me carefully as he said each word. I think he was especially tuned in to me with his last words. I admit, my eyebrows probably shot upward when I heard him say, 'and to help me remember.' I was prepared to be patient though and take his statement one piece at a time. "So, you truly believe that no matter what happens to you, EVERYTHING is here to serve you?" I needed to make sure he really meant this.

"Yes, all of life is beautiful and after 'practicing' this belief over the past six years I've discovered that within every single experience, large and small, there is a spiritual ecstasy involved. I feel a connection to the divine and know that everything that happens is a meaningful part of my plan here. It takes some time to see past my initial physically, emotionally and mentally preconceived notions, but the meaning and value are always there waiting for me. And each time I experience this wisdom it strengthens me for the next experience."

That sounded fantastic to me. I thought I was starting to get this and I wondered if I'd be able to do this in my life. I didn't want to get sidetracked just yet though. "Okay, I believe I understand what you've said so far, but Michael, what do you mean about 'helping you remember'? Remember what?" The way he'd watched me when he said it made it seem significant.

"Sam, this is another part of our 'practice' and a fundamental of our belief system. It requires a bit more background. Are you okay with that?"

"Sure," I said, "go for it."

133

"Well, Sam, we believe that each being on earth first existed in heaven and made a choice to come here. There is a lot more to it, but I want to cover the highlights before moving on to anything more complicated. While in heaven, each of us knew everything there was to know. We could answer any question, even before asking it. What we did not and could not do was 'experience' anything, because we had complete awareness of all. That is what earth provides, the opportunity to fully and completely 'experience' life. We get to choose everything. To see what it feels like to pick from any extreme or to make the same choices over and over again. Our gift of free will allows us to constantly choose whatever we desire and the further gift inherent in free will is that it is unrestricted and limitless. There are no penalties, punishments or conditions attached," said Michael.

"Hold on. Stop for a second please," I said. I had to stand up and move around while Michael spoke. This was too much for me to take in at once. I felt my head spinning a bit. This was all so new to me. It was like my conversations with Claire, except upped exponentially. And I think Michael actually said this wasn't the complicated explanation.

I could see Claire's expression. She looked concerned for me. She stood up and came over to me and put her arms around me. She whispered to me to breathe. It always came back to that. And so, I did. In and out, over and over, slower and slower. And when I was relaxed, she started speaking to me.

"Sam, I know you would benefit from a break. Let's go take a walk on the beach."

That sounded like a wonderful idea to me. Michael came over to me and asked if he could hug me. I told him 'yes'. His embrace was gentle and I could literally feel the peace he carried with him. It felt like some of it was rubbing off on me. I thanked him and then Claire and I headed off toward the sound of the waves.

There was something immensely comforting to me listening to wave after wave as they crashed on the shore.

"Sam, are you okay?"

"Better now," I said. "The ocean really does something for me. It quiets me like nothing else."

"Do you know why that is?", she asked.

"Not really," I answered, "it's just always been that way, ever since the first time I came here as a little boy. I feel like I belong here."

"You do Sam. We all do." Claire looked at me with her exquisite eyes. I felt pure love flowing out of her and into me. "Sam, imagine with me for a moment that heaven is like this ocean and that everyone here on earth was once a part of it, a part of its divine nature. Everyone a complete part of the whole. But because they wanted to 'experience' life separately, they chose to leave heaven and come to earth. And during the process of leaving, they chose to forget exactly what it was like in heaven so that they could fully 'experience' their earth life. But some part of them, their spirit essence, stays connected to heaven, even if they are not consciously aware of the connection. What Michael is telling you is that through the 'practice' that he and his tribe are committed to, they unveil the spiritual connection to the divine. They remember what it was like in heaven. They feel alive to the divine, inside them and beyond them."

I looked out at the ocean, imagining each sparkle as a single spiritual essence. It was beautiful, and her story was really appealing to me. But I wondered, if you made the decision to leave heaven so that you could fully 'experience' your earth life, why would you want to then 'remember' heaven? I thought about this for a few minutes but couldn't come up with anything, so I asked Little Buddha about it.

As was so often the case with her, instead of answering my question she asked me one of her own. "Sam, do you remember your 'heaven on earth' assignment?"

"Sure," I said, "that was awesome. I had a great time thinking through how I would want earth to be, to feel like my vision of heaven."

"Well, what was the 'feeling' you were trying to bring about?"

"There were a lot of them," I responded.

She looked at me. "But what was the most important one to you?"

I caught myself 'thinking' about the answer, then shifted into 'feeling'. It was so obvious as soon as I made the shift. "Love," I said.

"Yes, that's right. And that is what Michael is really talking about. Within each spiritual connection to the divine, love is created and revealed. It is always there, glorious and nourishing and sacred. It arises out of every experience and then becomes a part of who you are and overflows from inside of you to everyone and everything you touch. It goes far beyond this too. It reaches into the whole world and it guides us on our way home, flowing back to heaven."

Her revelation to me touched my heart so deeply. She wrapped her arms around me and I instantly knew what she was talking about. I felt a love so complete, so beautiful, so satisfying that I started to cry. They were tears of spontaneous joy. We stayed together for a while looking out at the ocean before returning to her cottage.

When we got back, Janine and Michael were waiting for us. Janine came over and looked up at me. She raised her right hand and placed it over my heart. She then lifted her left hand and in a sweeping motion brought it up close to her eyes and her heart and then rested it on top of her right hand, which was still over my heart. I knew what she was saying. "I love you, too," I said.

Little Buddha Book One

Claire spoke. "My mom has taken a vow of silence for a while, otherwise I think she would have wanted to contribute to our conversation. Her mom nodded, yes.

Wow! It wasn't until just now that I realized she hadn't spoken this whole time. I guess I really get absorbed at times. I wondered if some day that would change.

After Janine stepped aside, Michael came to stand facing me.

Michael's gaze was serene. He said, "Sam, may I share with you how my tribe says goodbye to each other after a profound event?"

"Absolutely," I said. "I'd love that."

"There are five lines. After I say one, you repeat it back to me, okay?"

"Yes, okay."

He looked directly into my eyes and said, "I see you."

It may sound strange but I 'felt' seen. We are so often preoccupied and don't even look each other in the eyes. Maybe we're afraid to see and be seen. I looked back at him and said, "I see you." It felt so good to acknowledge his presence in my life.

Michael then said, "I believe in your dreams," and I know he meant it. Both believed and was available to walk with me as I followed my dreams.

Because he'd told me so much about his 'practice' I felt I knew something about his dreams too. "I believe in your dreams," I told him.

"Even the ones you don't yet see," he said.

That felt really important to me because I was sure I had just scratched the surface of my dreams. There felt like there was so much more for me to experience and it was wonderful to know Michael recognized this. "Even the ones you don't yet see," I said back to him.

He smiled and said, "You mean something to me."

I had only just met him, but I knew without any doubt he meant this and I was overwhelmed. I managed to repeat, "You mean something to me," before I choked up a bit.

"You will be forever in my heart," Michael said as he placed the palm of his hands together and bowed to me.

I did the same, saying to him, "You will be forever in my heart."

I would have many conversations with Michael before he left to go home. My connection to him was so powerful, I could feel his presence even though he was a thousand miles away. What an enormous gift he is in my life.

one karma

Little Buddha Book One

one karma

It was a rare rainy day and Claire and I were sitting on her porch watching a pair of squirrels foraging in her yard.

She turned to me and said, "Let's do an art project." She told me she'd been dreaming about one that really had her inspired. In fact, she said, she'd already ordered part of the project and it should be ready to be picked up at a local art supply store. She reached for the phone, called and confirmed her order was in.

After telling her mom, we got in my car and headed out. Our first stop was the hardware store to buy a box of nails, some paintbrushes and paint. While we were shopping, one of the clerks came over to see if we needed help.

"How many different colors of paint do you have?", Little Buddha asked.

He considered, then responded, "We probably have over a thousand, since we got the new mixer." He watched her face illuminate and asked, "Will that be enough?" and laughed heartily.

"Actually," she said, "twenty-one will do nicely," smiling at him and enjoying his amusement.

He pointed to a series of color sample sheets and said, "Pick anything you like and let me know." After a moment, he asked, "What size do you want, a quart or a gallon?"

Claire selected twenty-one choices and told him that a quart each would work for our project.

He began mixing up her selections. "A project, huh? What are you making?" He seemed genuinely interested.

"I can't tell you yet because I'm going to surprise him," she said, pointing at me, "but you're certainly invited to come see it when we're done."

He smiled at her. "I'd like that little princess. Where do you live?"

I could tell this was all part of her plan. I don't know how she knew he'd be interested, but it didn't surprise me anymore when people just instantly warmed up to her.

Little Buddha Book One

"I live along alleyway number three, but you'll see a hand painted sign too saying, 'Moonlight Lane'. I'm the first cottage on the right. You know what they say, 'you can't miss it.'" She looked up at him and waited till he finished mixing the first quart and glanced down at her. Their eyes met, and I could see the profound change in his expression.

I'm not sure what exactly happened except that he stood very still and after maybe a whole minute, he said, "Thank you so much."

Little Buddha said, "It's my pleasure. Thank you so much for all of your assistance, then asked him, "Would it be okay if we came back for the paint later?"

"Sure," he said, "give me about an hour, in case I get interrupted by other customers."

"That sounds great. Thanks, Gus, we'll see you soon." We left and drove to the art supply store.

"Claire," I said, "How did you know his name was Gus?"

"Simple," she responded "it was on his name tag."

145

I was ready for this. "He wasn't wearing a name tag!"

"Oh well, I must have seen it another time and just remembered it."

I didn't believe this explanation, but I decided it really wasn't worth pursuing. I wondered if I would ever be able to 'know' things like she did without being told.

We arrived at the art store just as the rain stopped. It was a huge store, full of color and life. "This place is awesome," I said.

"I love it here, "Claire responded as she led me down the center aisle on our way to the back of the store. "The special-order desk is where we need to go for our pick up."

When we got there a male clerk was talking with an elderly woman. She seemed to be quite angry about something and was raising her voice to try to make a point. I saw Little Buddha reach out to touch her on the arm. As soon as she did, the woman's voice became softer and softer, until she was talking in a normal tone. I moved to the side so I could see the expression on her face. She looked calm and very peaceful. I whispered to Claire, "How did you do that?"

She pulled me down so she could whisper in my ear, "It's easy," she said, "It's all about exchanging energy."

I was pretty sure I'd need more of an explanation than that and decided I'd ask her later.

The woman finished her transaction and left, but not before smiling at Little Buddha and saying, "Thank you dear one."

Little Buddha told the clerk her name and asked for her order. He told her he'd be right back. When he returned, he was pushing a large hand truck with three big boxes balanced precariously on it. She paid him and he offered to help us load up my car. My curiosity was pretty high. What could she be up to?

After we were fully loaded, we went back to the hardware store. Gus was waiting for us and had all the paint mixed and boxed up. He also offered to carry them out to my car. It seemed as if everyone wanted to do us favors today. I wondered if that had anything to do either with her 'energy exchange' statement.

147

I was glad the rain had stopped because it took us a while to carry all her purchases into the cottage.

"Claire, I'm really curious, what's in the boxes?"

"Why don't you open them and see for yourself," she said, grinning.

I sliced open the tops of all three boxes and pulled the flaps back. Inside each were hearts cut out of wood. The hearts in each box were slightly different sizes. I guessed there were probably over three hundred. "Wow," I said, "there are so many."

"Three hundred and thirty-three, to be exact," Claire said. "I hope you like to paint."

"What's going on?", I asked, "are we really going to paint ALL of these?"

"Yes," she responded, "it's our summer art project. And after we paint them, we're going to hang them up on the outside of our alleyway fence so people can see them on their way to the beach. Won't that look fantastic?" She was beaming, so full of life and adventure.

"Yes, that will look fantastic," I agreed, "you'll probably get more people coming to your alleyway than any other on the beach."

"Well, let's get started, shall we?", she said, while clearing off her art table.

Although still keeping to her vow of silence, Janine came into the room, smiled at us and began arranging all the paint cans and brushes. I asked her if she was going to help us paint and she nodded a 'yes'. I really enjoyed spending time with her. I could see where Claire got a lot of her charm and enthusiasm. And her beauty.

Claire pulled out a few hearts from each box and set them down in front of each of us. Then the painting began in earnest. It was so much fun, and they all came out so differently. Janine laid a large tarp on the porch, and we used it as our staging area for the completed hearts.

As we worked, I asked Claire, "Can you tell me more about the exchange of energy you did today?"

Little Buddha Book One

She was finishing an intricate design on one of her hearts and said, "Sure, I'll tell you in a minute." I guessed I could wait that long.

Once she was done, she laid the heart aside and asked me, "Do you remember Michael telling you about the hidden energy that is attached to each one of our beliefs?"

"Sure," I said, "that was fascinating."

"Well this is similar. Everything in this life is made up of energy. All scientists know this, but they tend to concentrate on it from a structural point of view. There's so much more to it." She eyed me and asked, "How much do you want to know?"

Uh oh, I thought, that kind of question seemed pretty innocent, however, it probably meant I was going to have to work hard and pay close attention. But I'd learned over my years with her that everything she ever said was worth my hearing and worth my knowing. I told her, "Give it all to me."

"Okay," she said, "it all starts with heaven, where pure energy exists. The energy of heaven vibrates so fast it can't be seen. It's hard to explain but the energy is vibrating as 'pure love'. It encompasses everything and can be felt as pure bliss. Once an essence chooses to leave heaven, its energy frequency changes. It slows down. So much so that their physical form can be seen, the essence's earth form. And every essence has its own vibrational frequency. Actually, every physical part of them is vibrating at a different rate. And how each part vibrates, in relationship to its whole, determines its state of health. When certain parts are vibrating out of harmony, the body experiences what we usually call 'disease'. And bringing the body back into harmony can be very challenging for people."

"Wait a second," I said, "give me a chance to assimilate this. I've never heard anyone explain anything like this. Okay, so everything is made of energy and once we 'arrive' here on earth it has slowed down enough so that we can see it as a person. Wow, this is pretty incredible. So, were Gus and the angry woman at the art store both 'out of balance' and you did something to change that?", I asked.

"Yes," she responded. "I've become very sensitive to when other people's energy is, I'll call it, 'troubled'. When I sense this I can offer them a gift of love, which is pure energy. They can reject or accept it, as they choose, because free will is working all of the time. There doesn't have to be a 'conversation' about it, they just sense it is there for them and they can choose to take it in."

"I watched both of them and saw how quickly they changed and became calm and happy. It was amazing."

"People do this all the time. I've seen you do it too. It's a natural part of who we are. It's the degree to which we are conscious of the exchange that's different among people."

"Do you mean some people are intentional about it?", I asked.

"Yes, it's one of the things Mom and I love to teach each other."

That statement said so much to me about their relationship. It was true, I'd witnessed them talking about all sorts of things, one teaching the other about what they'd discovered, without regard to their age. It was really special. I wondered if it could be like that for everyone? Our culture seemed so set regarding so many things and kids sharing their wisdom didn't seem to be one of them.

I still wanted to know one more thing about this idea of an 'energy exchange'. "Claire, I think I understand that you somehow get in touch with the energy, the pure love inside of you and then choose to share it with someone who appears to you to need it, but what do you get back from them?" The idea of 'exchange' seemed incomplete without my knowing the answer to this.

"I think I understand why you are confused," she answered. "You probably are assuming that I receive something from them in return for my 'gift', right?"

"Yes," I said, confirming her assumption.

"I'm sorry Sam," she said, eager to clear up what she meant. "The 'gift' I offer is from heaven. I've opened up through my spirit and asked to receive pure energy, pure love, so that I may offer it to someone in need. What they receive is not 'from me', but 'through me'. The same is true for them. If they accept the 'gift' of pure energy, it transforms their current 'troubled' energy, changing it into pure love. They have chosen to exchange a lesser energy for a greater energy."

"Can anyone do this?", I asked.

Little Buddha Book One

"Yes, anyone."

I needed to think about this before I asked any more questions. There were some incredible ramifications here and my mind was a little on overload.

We went back to painting our hearts. It was more fun than I'd expected. The variety, style and color choices were so different among the three of us.

I had another question cross my mind. I remembered Michael talking about our physical, emotional, mental and spiritual make up and then he focused a bit on our ego. He said it was a very important part of us. I personally found it to be quite challenging, both mine and the ego of others.

I looked over at Claire and asked, "Can you tell me more about ego?"

She glanced up at her mom and smiled. "Well, mom has talked with me a lot about it, so I'll tell you what she told me."

"Much of our suffering lies within our ego's misperceptions. The ego is tied to our physical, emotional and mental states and

154

believes that its strength and satisfaction come from these. But the truth is that our strength and satisfaction come when we are connected to our source, through our spirit and our heart. When we believe we are nourished through our physical self, like our wealth, possessions and talents or our intellectual self, through our thinking mind and interpersonal connections or through our emotional self and all of our feelings, then we will always fight to protect these sources. We will be afraid that we will lose the things we feel we 'need' and will constantly live in a state of fear. This will happen until we recognize and know that these are not our sources of power. Nothing our ego touches is. If we stop and go inside ourselves, we will see that our connection to source, our spiritual source, is what provides for our support and happiness. It is our source of love and our true home."

I thought for a moment, this makes so much sense to me now. "Thank you both for your wisdom," I said, bowing to each of them. "I guess my experience has been that I feel my ego has been more enemy than friend."

"Sam," Little Buddha said, as she looked up from her current heart painting, "do you remember Michael telling you about 'good' and 'bad' labels and how they immediately alter your experience?"

"Sure, that's been really important for me to keep in mind," I responded.

"Well, using 'enemy' and 'friend' in relation to your ego, is doing the same thing. Do you see how this would be true?"

As a matter of fact, I did, as soon as she said it out loud. "Yes, and it probably works for any kind of label, doesn't it?"

Claire and Janine both nodded.

It was so delightful to spend time with them. I always felt so accepted and loved by them. I hoped I could be that way for others in my life.

It was lunchtime and we were all hungry. Janine was the first to move off to the kitchen. Claire and I looked over our masterpieces. They were really beautiful, especially when you saw them altogether. I was really feeling the joy of creation.

After lunch Claire and I decided to take a walk along one of the trails close to their cottage. It led to a gorgeous little freshwater pond with a small stretch of sand beach. On our way, I decided to ask another question. I seemed so full of them these days. Claire never seemed to mind, no matter how many I came up with.

I'd been bothered by the whole idea of karma. I'd heard all different versions, some of them pretty disconcerting to me. The worst one said that you'd be punished for every 'bad' thing you'd ever done. That was scary to me because even though I didn't think I'd done a lot of 'bad' things, I wasn't sure who got to rate them and what the punishments would be. I supposed that god would be the judge, but some folks said it didn't have anything to do with god, it was just the way life worked. I wanted to know what Claire thought, so I asked her about it once we arrived at the pond.

She told me to pick up three stones; a small, a medium and a large one. Then she asked me to wade out a little into the pond and stand there. So, I did. After a minute or two the water's surface was as smooth as glass and picked up the reflections of everything surrounding it.

"Now throw the largest stone and tell me what happens," she said.

157

I heaved the largest stone away from me and there was a loud splash followed by circular ripples coming from where it fell in. It felt kind of funny that she wanted me to tell her what happened, when she could see for herself, but this was my question and the way she wanted me to answer. So, I said, "The stone hit the surface, splashed, sank and created ripples that moved out in all directions."

"Good. Now throw the medium stone and tell me what happens."

I held the medium stone, then tossed it in the same direction and then described out loud the result. "It made a smaller splash and the ripples still went in circles in all directions, but slower than the first."

"Okay, now throw the smallest stone and tell me what happens."

I threw it easily and of course the same thing happened. "Well, it made a pretty small splash and small ripples that are taking a comparatively long time to reach me," I called out. I confess I was thinking to myself, what does this have to do with karma? You would think by now I would know better.

Little Buddha Book One

I heard her ask, "Is it possible for the ripples to bypass you or is it the course of nature that they go right through you?"

"They go right through me," I responded, "since I'm standing in their way." I felt like adding, 'duh?' to my answer, but I knew she was trying to teach me something important. Something I'd asked her.

"Sam, karma is very simple. You throw a stone, it hits the water, it creates ripples, the ripples come back to you. That's it. There is no moral to the story. There is no judgment involved. There is an action and a reaction. Do you understand?"

Sure, that sounded pretty simple. I got it. "Yes," I said, "but…"

Little Buddha held up her hand to stop me. "Sam, you want more, right?"

I nodded, 'Yes'.

And so, she asked me, "Answer me this, what creates karma?" She studied my face and added, "Use our example of the ripples."

I thought back to the three splashes and answered, "Karma is created as a result of the stones hitting the water."

"No," she said, "think deeper."

Okay, deeper. "Karma is created by the act of throwing the stones."

"No," she said, "think deeper."

So, I thought some more, now 'deeper' and 'harder' and wondered what is before the act of throwing? "Karma is created by the thought about throwing the stones," I said. That had to be it. I looked at her expectantly.

"Almost there," she said, "think even deeper."

"I'm sorry, I'm all out of ideas," I told her. Really what else could there be left?

"Well," she laughed, "that's what they make nights for, for thinking about answers to questions."

That surely was the case for me, I thought.

Little Buddha Book One

After finishing our walk and some more painting, we all decided to 'call it a day'. After all, I had some thinking to do tonight.

On the next morning, I came through her gate and I had nothing. No amount of thinking had produced a better guess than the three from yesterday.

She could tell by the look on my face the moment she saw me.

"Don't worry," she said, "this wasn't a test to pass or fail. It was just an opportunity for you to reach a bit toward an answer you wanted."

"Could you just please tell me the answer?", I pleaded.

"Sam, the essence of karma and its creation is all about 'intention'. In the pond, the ripples are the natural result of the stone hitting the water, and in life, our intentions create their own kind of ripples, which always come back to us. Our intention is the spark of creation and the animating force of life, bringing all things into being. Our intention precedes every choice we make and brings about every shift in our awareness. It inspires every thought, word and action." She paused for a moment. "When our intention is love, it is love that ripples back to us. The greater your love, the greater it is returned to you. This is true for everything you put out into your world. So, if it is your 'desire', your 'choice', to live a life of love, center on that intention and it will be yours."

I closed my eyes and just stood still. A smile crept across my face. I understood what she was telling me. There was some pure joy happening inside of me. I opened my arms, and she came and hugged me. How's that for a ripple, I thought

going deeper (exercises)

Little Buddha Book One

going deeper
(exercises)

I want to offer you an opportunity to go deeper into the stories, so the following sections provide a suggestion for focus, an opening prayer/meditation and some questions to consider. Hopefully this will be helpful for those who would like to spend some time in self-study or perhaps, for group study and discussion.

forgiveness
opportunity for going deeper:

This story centered on forgiveness. Is there someone you feel a need or desire to forgive in your life? Perhaps, you would like to be forgiven by someone else or maybe you would like to forgive yourself for something you've done or left undone. Consider spending a little time and coming up with a forgiveness focus for this time of going deeper.

Little Buddha Book One

forgiveness
opening prayer/meditation

Imagine you've fallen into a deep, wonderful sleep. Imagine images now appear. They are beautiful, peaceful, graceful. Your awareness takes everything in without any effort on your part. There is music surrounding you, lifting you, supporting you. The music is more than sound, it is color also, moving and washing over you. As one moment flows into the next, you sense a gradual loss of being separate. You are vibrating in harmony with everything and the bliss builds inside of you. You are merging with your "dream" world. There is a sense of oneness, of knowingness. You are becoming awareness. You realize every answer without having had to ask any questions. You sense the truth. You know the truth. That love is all there is. All there ever will be. Every image that had held you from this truth has disappeared. Rest here for a moment. (pause) See this and feel this and remember this. It is a gift to you.

Amen.

Little Buddha Book One

forgiveness
(questions)

Have you ever watched a child investigate their world? If so, what did you notice?

Has anyone ever surprised you with an answer to a question you asked? What happened?

Do you believe that all of the thoughts and feeling you have, YOU chose to 'put there' (to keep inside of you)?

Do you think it's possible that others are 'full' and don't have 'any room left' for anything else, like Claire said?

Do you believe that forgiveness could 'open up some space' inside of you?

Would you be willing to try the 'forgiveness process'? If not, what would prevent you?

What keeps you from forgiving (others or yourself)?

How do you think it would be to be brought up as a child being able to release things that no longer serve you?

Does it seem possible to you that a six-year old could be this wise? Are you open to learning from others, regardless of their age?

connecting the dots
opportunity for going deeper:

In this story, although Sam did not initially understand, he came to recognize the value of 'connecting the dots'. Spend a few moments and think about some of the events of your life. Which ones would you like to understand better? Choose one and see if you can use the process Little Buddha shared with Sam to find meaning in connecting your dots.

Little Buddha Book One

connecting the dots
opening prayer/meditation

Imagine this is YOUR prayer. It holds within it all the things you want to say to god. Perhaps at first it is what your head needs to say.

Imagine emptying yourself of everything that presents a challenge to you or confuses you or angers you. Everything that your mind cannot reconcile or comprehend. You decide to let it ALL go. A part of you watches this beautiful emptying. A serene peace fills you. Rest here for a moment. (pause)

Now from this place, imagine allowing your heart to speak to you. Welcome its words and feelings, like they were a long lost and much loved friend.

What do you hear from this pure heart? Can you hear it calling you into the open, encouraging you to expand into your fullness? Allow yourself to breathe in the beauty of this, to feel the essence of love surrounding you, being you. Rest in this place. (pause)

Little Buddha Book One

In this inner heart space, softly look around you. Notice you are connected with everyone and everything. What appeared to you as separate, no longer is separate from you. You are a glorious part of the one. Effortlessly your heart feels a divine sense of gratefulness, peacefulness and love. This is your home.

Breathe in the air here. Fill yourself all the way up. Feel the smile that you are. Take a moment and truly feel this place. (pause)

And now imagine carrying this 'home' in the very center of you- today and every day. Your heart always knows this is who you are.

Amen.

Little Buddha Book One

connecting the dots
questions

Is there anyone in your life who seems to 'know' things that surprise you? How do you think they do it?

Do you think there is a 'plan' for your life? If so, how do you think it works?

What do you think about what Michael says, "That everything we think, feel or say is either from fear or from love"?

How do you feel about what Michael says, "That fear is not real, that it is there for us to push against and to point the way toward love"?

How do you feel about Michael's statement about illness, "So if we choose to fight our condition, like sickness, we are feeding it fear and this always creates conflict and when your energy is already low, any kind of fighting works against you"?

Have you ever noticed that when you are sick and forced to slow down, you can see things differently?

What examples are there in your life where there are dots that can be connected?

What do you think it would feel like to see the 'dots' as they happen, rather than in retrospect?

What are your thoughts about everyone's dots being connected?

What would the picture of your life look like if it were a 'connect the dots' picture?

heaven on earth
opportunity for going deeper:

Sam accepted Claire's assignment to write down what his version of 'heaven on earth' would look like. It was a challenging task for him. Write down your ideas of what heaven would look like to you. If you want to, share this with someone else in your life.

Little Buddha Book One

heaven on earth
opening prayer/meditation

Have you ever wondered what life would be like without limits? Those others have chosen for us and those we've accepted for ourselves?

What might life be like if we could release certain words? Words like DON'T and CAN'T and SHOULDN'T. What if we let their power over us fall away?

Imagine what beautiful things might happen. Imagine giving breath to this idea and filling it with hope...like filling a hot air balloon so you could soar off into the sky.

What if we decided it was okay to move beyond our current limits? In fact, while we're at it, how about we raise the bar from OKAY to it being FANTASTIC? How wonderful would it feel to live with an open mind and open eyes and an open heart? How about we take the training wheels off our dreams?

Can you feel the freedom?

Little Buddha Book One

Can you imagine what it would be like if all of your existing thoughts were no longer attached so securely? Instead what if they were easy to peel away so we could have room for new ideas?
Can you feel the liberation in this?

This life is up to each of us, formed by all our choices and decisions. Our prayer, mother, father god is to be open to all of our possibilities and our grandest vision. Thank you for making it so.

Amen.

Little Buddha Book One

heaven on earth
questions

What do you want most from your life?

How often do you use the word "should"? How does it make you feel? Have you ever considered exchanging it for the words, "What would benefit me"?

Little Buddha says she reminds herself every day that she is "part of god, whole and complete and not missing anything." Who do you think you really are?

When you are upset by something, do you remember to slow down, breathe and feed yourself love?

What is your morning spiritual routine?

Do you believe you can have anything you desire? Why or why not?

What do you think of Claire's statement that "Life isn't a race, it's a journey toward bliss"?

Would you like to be able to tell others that you love them, without it being awkward or uncomfortable?

Little Buddha Book One

What do you think about Sam's "heaven on earth" list?

If Claire had given you the "heaven on earth" assignment, what would you have included?

the inner path-beginning
opportunity for going deeper:

Claire indicates to Sam that although he's accepted that the world outside of him is where he believes wisdom exists, that the opposite is true. She tells him that everything of importance is already within him. Spend a few minutes in meditation and see what your inner wisdom tells you. Write down what you receive.

Little Buddha Book One

the inner path-beginning
opening prayer/meditation

Imagine a tree lined country road stretching out in front of you with wonderful long branches arching over you as you walk.

The air is fresh and the sun warm, as it filters through the leaves and onto your face.

Your breathing is slow and easy. It is a dream of a day.

You are approaching a bridge crossing a magnificent stream. You're caught up in the beauty and completely miss seeing the branch lying across the road.

You stumble and just catch yourself before falling.

You wonder how it is possible that you did not see the branch in the middle of your path.

And you notice how this is a metaphor for life.

How often you've tripped over debris, some of it you realize is of your own making.
You feel the pain it causes and wonder why?
Why do we create suffering of this kind?

Little Buddha Book One

Is there a message inside of this pain?

There is a voice which often speaks in a whisper, so quiet you have to be very still to hear it.

It speaks truth to you, telling you that all pain and all suffering is a call to awareness. A chance to choose, to center in on happiness and love. To spread joy and kindness.

And so, you take the branch and fashion it into a walking stick, something to take with you as a reminder, that how you view the world is up to you each step of the way.

Amen.

Little Buddha Book One

the inner path-beginning
questions

Sam seems determined to put limits on himself. Do you feel you do this same thing? If so, how?

What did you think when Sam and Little Buddha were talking about "pointing the way" versus "showing the way"?

What do you think about the cave analogy?

Do you trust "outside" wisdom (from the world) more than "inside" wisdom (from inside yourself)? Why?

Who are you most like in the story of searching for water; the farmer, the diviner or the sons and why?

What do you believe about your "inner path" and does it lead you to wisdom and awareness?

What do you think of Little Buddha's statement, "I know that you've been told that wisdom is a process of acquisition, but I'm telling you, it is the opposite. My inner path has become a beautiful process of release of all my assumptions about everything. As I let go, what I realize is that there is a divine wisdom at my very core. As I release what I 'think' I know, I can 'feel' the truth."?

What are your thoughts and feelings about Little Buddha's statement, "Do you remember my telling you that we know everything but we chose to forget so that we could fully experience this world? Well, this may not sound important, but it is. It's the key to everything. Hidden inside of you is every answer you could ever want or need. To move from the outside to the inside releases every limit and opens the whole world to you. Choosing to remember is like turning on the flashlight when you are in the cave of darkness."?

Claire says to Sam, "Imagine you're sitting comfortably in a chair looking out at the ocean. You see the surf rolling toward and landing on the beach and feel the warmth of the sun. You see the gulls soaring and spinning through the air and hear their piercing cries. You're totally absorbed in this scene unaware that there is a thin veil between all that you see and another truth that exists. A truth, that beyond your earth perceptions there is a divine space, a place you know even better than this world. A place you first called home, a space called 'heaven'. Allow yourself the freedom to feel this place and rest here for a minute. Allow yourself to remember. Feel your heart open and fill with joy. Stay right here and feel refreshed and renewed." What do you "feel" inside of you about this statement?

Do you believe you can find your way "home" using this meditation? If you ASK for help, do you believe an answer will be given to you?

the bug box
opportunity for going deeper:

Claire gently captures bugs from inside her house and releases them outside so that they can continue living. The next time you see a bug inside your home, gently capture it and release it outdoors. How does this make you feel?

the bug box
opening prayer/meditation

I try to listen carefully to god. This is what I heard recently. "Tell them I believe in liberation and freedom from all expectations, for expectations are a human invention. I have no set expectations and I find no real value in them. Expectations and demands cause suffering and if you create them but don't meet them you will feel yourself a failure, and I do not believe in failure. I tell you now what I believe in. YOU. Every one of you. We are totally and completely connected by love. It is a love that bridges all of your perceived failures, because they are just that, your perceptions. There are no real failures and therefore there is no necessary suffering. I love you, before, during and after every action you take, every feeling you experience and every thought that moves through you. There is nothing you will ever do that will separate us. I would like you to remember this because that can end this kind of suffering."

Remember I love you, always and forever.

Amen

Little Buddha Book One

the bug box
questions

How would it feel to you to receive a handwritten letter in a beautifully designed envelope?

What does Little Buddha's statement, "The essence of every wisdom is alive in the universe", mean to you?

Although thinking is valuable, Little Buddha says that "feelings" are what is most important. What do you think she means? What do you believe?

Sam shares about the conditioning he received from the world. How were you conditioned during your childhood?

When Sam arrives at Little Buddha's cottage she hugs him and he feels like he's "been embraced by heaven". Is there anyone in your life that hugs you like that?

Little Buddha challenges Sam about making assumptions instead of asking. What happens in your life when you make assumptions?

Little Buddha Book One

Have you ever "rescued" a bug of any kind? How did that feel?

Little Buddha says to Sam, "There are no right answers, there is only your answer". What do you think about this statement?

Do you make a practice of asking your heart questions? If yes, what is it like for you and if not, what prevents you from asking?

Little Buddha tells Sam there are no limits and that every single thing is possible. Is this possible for you to believe? Why?

the room
opportunity for going deeper:

In order to experience some of what Sam did, make a commitment to performing a certain number of "intentional acts of kindness" and record what your thoughts and feelings are about the project.

Little Buddha Book One

the room
opening prayer/meditation

It feels true to me that each of us is blessed with the gift of choice. It is not always a welcome gift. It seems to come with an implied responsibility. We choose and then we receive the fruits of the choice. Sometimes we don't like the fruits. They seem bitter and hard to swallow. We may often wonder, is there a better way to make choices? Are we being unrealistic to expect that each of our choices will bear delicious fruit?

There are lots of times we may be unsure what the best choice even is. What do we do then? We may not be exactly sure why it is so difficult for us to remember that there is a better way, because there is. We can choose to ask spirit for loving guidance. We can turn inward, into our depth and listen for god's words to us. We all have this same choice. It is so beautiful to know that mother, father god loves us and is always there for us, for whatever we need. We may choose to be grateful to be reminded that although we have power to make ALL of our own choices, one of them can be to ask for god's love and support. Amen.

Little Buddha Book One

the room
questions

Sam asks Claire what it will be like for him when he's dead. What do you believe happens? What will it look like for you?

Claire tells Sam that when he dies, "It will be as you choose it to be." What do you think about her statement?

Claire says to Sam, "god wants what you want." How do you feel about this?

Claire also tells Sam, "You have the free will to choose anything and it will be as you see it." Sam responds that he's been taught that he's "required" to do what god wants. What do you think about these two statements? What were you taught?

Little Buddha tells Sam he has free will to choose anything without requirement, expectation, obligation or repercussion. What is your opinion about this? Do you have this opinion because you've been taught it or is it your own conclusion?

How do you think it would be to be able to re-live any event from your past?

Which one would you pick first? Are there ones you'd be afraid to re-live?
Have you ever performed "intentional acts of kindness"? What did you do? What were the reactions you received?

Imagine for a second that you are god...what do you want?

Claire says, "You see Sam, each of us is a part of god, each able to choose our own path. If it is our desire to experience fear and a feeling of separation, we know inside ourselves what choices to make and if we want to experience love and unity, we also know deep inside, what choices will bring this into our lives. Free will is the gift you choose with." How do you feel about Claire's statement? Do you think it is true?

a million of you
opportunity for going deeper:

Imagine that you are talking with Claire and she asks you to accept the same challenge she gave to Sam, to observe a tree for a week. Consider accepting and spending time with a tree (or something else you feel could be important to you) and writing down what happens during the week (or even one day).

Little Buddha Book One

a million of you
opening prayer/meditation

I invite you to close your eyes and let your heart softly open.

I wonder if your heart ever asks you questions. Does it sense that you dream of making some changes, that your life, your heart wishes to open, to be free, to fill and overflow with love? Or does it hold back, uncertain and afraid, unsure of what will happen? Does it wonder what it would be like if your world was bigger, wider, fuller?

Mine does and the question becomes, where does the faith come from to make this happen? You might want to know before you leap. But this is not possible, because part of knowing is believing.

Just for a moment, accept in the deepest place inside of you that every imaginable possibility exists, and that there is an answer to every question, a peace for every concern, a love for every fear. Feel the beauty of this. Realize that where you are right in this moment is the state of conception.

Little Buddha Book One

Everything is possible, every direction open, every choice available. It is from this very place that every change happens. An act of conception gives birth to every action and life is made real, made into a divine experience.

So, in this moment, ask what your heart truly desires...hold this space open and listen carefully...and if something comes, embrace it and hold it close to you...breathe life into it, for it has come to show you love...and to open your life.

If nothing comes right away, remember your way back to this place and ask again.

Thank you, mother, father god, divine spirit, for the world of conception and the believing that creates our life, our world, our experience.

Amen

Little Buddha Book One

a million of you
questions

What is the longest book or book series you've ever read? Can you imagine reading the whole Encyclopedia Britannica as a nine- year old?

Have you ever thought about Claire's statement that facts don't always stay as facts and that the truth appears to change depending on who you're talking with?

What do you think about Claire's statement that, "You can only know your own truth"?

How do you feel about Claire's statement to Sam that "The biggest barrier to learning anything is thinking you already know about it"? Does that feel true to you?

Have you ever spent time observing some part of nature for any length of time? What were your observations?

Have you ever "sensed" something (like Sam "feeling" the same energy in the acorn as in the whole oak tree) about a part of nature you had no logical explanation for?

Little Buddha Book One

Do you think it is possible to have a "conversation" with a tree or other part of nature? Has this ever happened to you or someone you know? How do you explain this?

What do you think about the idea of each of us having "spiritual DNA", a blueprint for our earth life already within us when we are born?

Can you imagine that there are an unlimited number of images of you and you can experience any one of them? And that it is your free will that determines the choice?

Claire tells Sam that to experience his limitlessness he can use the formula of "conceive, believe and act". Have you ever tried this? How has it worked for you?

outside inside
opportunity for going deeper:

Here's an art project to try if you'd like. Using white paper of any size, draw something that has many offshoots (the sun and its rays, a tree and its branches and roots, a field with many flowers). Feel free to use as many colors as you like. Once the picture is drawn, write down all the things you can think of that nourish you along the offshoots. Feel freedom with this. Spelling and color choices are up to you. See what it feels like to recognize how many different things support and nourish you.

Little Buddha Book One

outside inside
opening prayer/meditation

What is the measure of any of us? Perhaps it is the reflection of us? Do we love? Are we loved? Does our heart pour outward? Are we a gift and a giver? Each of us can look outside ourselves for this reflection, but the truer measure is what we see on the inside.

However, at times, our sight is too cloudy, as if a mist makes everything unclear. At these times, it helps to use others' eyes, to hear others' words and use another's heart to hear the beating of our own.

When I stand close to others, I sometimes feel their suffering from unnecessary judgment. Sometimes I am familiar with the source of this judgment and I see what it does to their spirit. It weighs heavily, smothering each and every lightness. And every expectation, born from our perception of what others want or need or demand or require from us, turns our inner whiteness to gray and black.

It doesn't have to be this way. Very little has to happen to change this. A mere few words. Easy to say..."I let go." I let go of each and every thought that feels heavy. No matter what is happening in or around me, I know what feels heavy. And, thank god, I am in charge of me. And I can say, "I release you" to every heavy thought. I know this means I will have to repeat this message to myself over and over and over again. All of what created this idea that I must or should accept this heaviness, as what life requires of me, came about over time. I reinforced it till it became natural to me. So now I would benefit from knowing that it is MY choice what to do now. Somehow, I have accepted things the way they are, even though they cause me suffering. If I look, I can see how easily certain things in my life cause suffering. And they all have two things in common. They come from fear and they are healed by love. So how do I help myself, knowing this is my truth?

By remembering. Remembering what my truth is, that there is truly only LOVE. It is the source of all things. It was here before the world came into being. It is here now and forever. Love's truth is that it is all there is and all there ever will be. You are made of this love. It is the only way you could ever have come into existence. It is who you are by your very nature. Everything else you experience has been added. Everything. Many of these things are valuable, but sometimes there are things that create doubt and hurt and criticism of our own image. We profit from knowing they are not real. The only real thing is love. I benefit from realizing that I came here from love and I will return to love. I do not ever have to prove to anyone else or to myself that I am worthy of love because it is who I already am. I believe, I feel this as my truth and your truth.

Amen.

outside inside
questions

Do you think everything is possible? If not, what is not possible? What limits your beliefs?

Have you ever experienced something you'd previously thought was impossible? What shifted in your outlook for this to happen?

Do you believe you experience limits because that's what you are telling yourself?

What provides you with a sense of safety and security?

Do you feel you need to be in "control" to feel safe and secure? How many things do you think are under your direct control?

Do you feel very little is under your direct control or that it takes too much time and energy to constantly maintain control? If so, are you open to a new approach?

When you are speaking with someone do you look at them (their face, their eyes)? Do you think they can tell they are important to you? Does anyone in your life do this for you?

What would you write down if you did the "assignment" Claire gave to Sam about listing under two columns, your "inside validations" and your "outside validations"?

Take a look at your list and see which validations comes from fear and which come from love

If you drew a sun picture with rays going out in all directions, what would you put on each ray that represents things that nourish you?

the practice
opportunity for going deeper

Sit back for a minute and close your eyes and relax. Imagine you are reviewing your life. Events pop up. Choose one and release any label of good or bad that is attached. Sit with the event and see if you can "feel" what energy is attached to it. Does the energy feel like it comes from fear or love? See if you can release the power of fear and embrace the power of love. Does it shift the way you feel about the event? Can you sense the spiritual ecstasy that the power of love creates?

Little Buddha Book One

the practice
opening prayer/meditation

I invite you to close your eyes and encourage your body to relax, taking one breath in and letting it out... slowly. And again.

Take a moment to remind yourself about the truth, that you are a divine child of god, from both mother and father spirit. You are beautiful and unique and special.

Open wide to know that you can ask for anything. Any question, any request. Everything is open to you.

Mother, Father is always with you, alive in every moment of your life. Present in every heartbeat. You already know this in your heart but sometimes not in your head.

At times, there are other voices. Ones that confuse you and offer doubts about your divine connection. It is the world speaking to you.

That's okay. You live here now. Live with every imaginable choice. Able to move every possible direction and pursue any dream.

Little Buddha Book One

What do you choose? Is it your desire to experience a life of happiness and joy? To feel fully alive? Are you ready to wake up?

Do you wonder how this can be done?

Divine spirit answers this way...live from the inside out. Live from your heart, from your center of love, first for yourself, your holy, beautiful self. And from here you can extend outward, giving from your abundance of love to others and to the world.

And as it always is, from giving comes receiving.

Take a moment and drink this wisdom in. And now open your eyes and know we are one. Look around you and see and feel the love you create, shining in everyone.

Amen.

Little Buddha Book One

the practice
questions

Have you ever met someone and felt an immediate connection? If so, why do you suppose that was?

Have you ever considered something "negative" that happened to you (lost physical or mental abilities) to be a "gift"? If yes, what made it so for you?

What do you think of Michael's statement to Sam about his belief system, "Everything I experience is a gift. It is something I've brought into my world to expand my awareness. The only time it ever becomes difficult is if I forget and label the experience 'bad' or 'good'. Whenever that happens it makes it very hard to remain open to the message, because I've already decided the meaning, before I've had a chance to actually see what it has to share with me"?

What do you believe the difference is between what you "think" about something and how you "feel" about it?

What "things" in your life have become "second nature" to you? How did they get that way?

Do you label things in your life "good" and "bad"? How would your experience of life change if you didn't label them and accepted them just as a part of your earth experience?

How do you feel about Michael's statement to Sam that Sam's job loss may have "appeared" to come from "outside" of him, but didn't, it came from "inside" of him? That it is somehow a part of his earth "plan"? If this is challenging for you, is it possible for you to shift your belief system to consider this?

What do you think about the idea of "spiritual DNA"?

How do you feel about the concept of "hidden energy"? Try picking one belief you have and sitting quietly with it and see what kind of energy is attached to it.

Do you believe that every experience you have provides you with something of value?

What do you think of Claire's explanation to Sam about each spirit essence "choosing" to come to earth and going through the "great forgetting", so that they won't already "know" everything?

one karma
opportunity for going deeper:

Here's another art project. Think about the people in your life and choose one you'd like to give a gift to. Take a sheet of white paper and colored pencils or markers and draw a picture for them. While drawing, be attentive to the "intention" inside of you. What are you "feeling" about the person who will receive your picture? Is it love? Do you believe the energy of love becomes a part of the drawing?

Little Buddha Book One

one karma
opening prayer/meditation

Imagine that inside of you there is silence. It is peaceful, blissful. Allow an anticipation to grow inside of you. Know that something very special is about to enter your world.

And now you hear it. It is the voice of the divine, asking to speak to you.

Give your heart permission to open and allow yourself to say YES. Yes, please come to me.

The voice is pure, warm, soothing, radiant. And a profound peace moves through your whole body. Every part of you vibrates with a sacred rhythm.

And because your heart has offered its open invitation, divine words enter into you.

And here is what is said: "I wanted you to know I have such love for you. Some part of you may think you are not worthy, this is untrue, it is merely an image others have told you. I tell you the real truth. We are as one. I am love and so too, you are love, whole complete and perfect."

"I sense you might not see this right now. It will be as you choose, but this perception is not reality, not my reality."

"Take the wise path, and let this perception go, and allow all other limitations to be set free, and drift away. And remember, you mean everything to me. I live for you and I live within you, always in your next breath, your next heartbeat, your next divine smile. I came here, in this moment, to be with you. To tell you, I love you beyond any measure of the word. And I want you to know in your heart that I love you NOW AND FOREVER."

Amen.

Little Buddha Book One

one karma
questions

Do you know anyone who seems to just know things, like Claire knowing Gus's name in the story? If so, how do you think they do it?

Have you ever seen someone "calm" someone else down by just touching them? Has anyone ever done that to you?

Have you ever done a big art project just for fun? If you gave yourself the time, what project would you choose?

Before explaining about energy exchange Claire asks Sam, "How much do you want to know"? If you could know how life really works, how much would you want to know?

What do you think about Claire's statement to Sam that heaven's energy is "pure love" and that once an essence chooses to leave heaven its frequency slows to the point where it can be seen as a physical form?

How do you feel about the idea that each part of our body has an optimal vibrational frequency and when it is not at this frequency, we experience a condition we refer to as "disease"?

Do you believe it is possible, as Claire says, to be able to offer a "gift" of pure love to others and that they can either accept or reject it using their free will?

Claire tells Sam that she and her mother, Janine, teach each other about energy exchanges. Would you say you've learned many things from children? What lessons do you remember?

What do you think about Claire's response to Sam's question about how the exchange works when Claire says, "The 'gift' I offer is from heaven. I've opened up through my spirit and asked to receive pure energy, pure love, so that I may offer it to someone in need. What they receive is not 'from me', but 'through me'. The same is true for them. If they accept the 'gift' of pure energy, it transforms their current 'troubled' energy, changing it into pure love. They have chosen to exchange a lesser energy for a greater energy"?

How do you feel about Claire's statement that our strength and satisfaction come when we are connected to our source, meaning our spiritual source?

Do you feel that all sources of nourishment, based on our physical, emotional and mental selves, ultimately make us fearful because they can all be taken away from us?

How do you feel about what Claire says, that it is only when we go inside to our spiritual source that we will find what provides for our support and strength?

What do you feel is the role of the ego?

What have you been told about "karma" during your life? What do you believe?

How do you feel about Little Buddha's answer to Sam that what creates karma is our "intention", which she calls the "spark of creation"?

Little Buddha Book One Notes

Little Buddha Book One

Made in the USA
Middletown, DE
02 July 2017